Historic Houses & Gardens

by Trevor Fisher
with sketches by
Malcolm Newall

The development and character of historic houses in the West Midlands, Shropshire and Staffordshire, with notes on access, transport and facilities.

****

Quercus
John Roberts
8 Hillside Close, Bartley Green
Birmingham B32 4LT
****

Historic Houses & Gardens
(Shropshire, Staffordshire & West Midlands)

by Trevor Fisher
with sketches by
Malcolm Newell

ISBN 1 898136 11 4

First Published 1996

Preface

Quercus is a regional publisher specialising in books about the western Midlands, or the area that geographers call the "Midland Triangle". This is the land between the three great rivers - Trent, Severn and Avon, which can be seen as a physical entity. This is very relevant to our two books about the Midlands countryside, *Midland Woods & Forests* and *Midland Rivers,* much more so than the old division into shire counties. Since the triangle is also to some extent a social and economic entity, it is a useful way of defining an area for books such as *Midland Ghosts & Hauntings, Midland Castles* and this one. It will will also apply to the forthcoming *Midland Murders & Mysteries, Coaching Days in the Midlands* and *Midland Spirits & Spectres.*

It was *Midland Castles* by Mike Salter which first prompted Trevor Fisher to approach me with a proposal for a similar book on country houses. After much discussion we decided that for reasons of work pressures and the size (and cost) of such a book, it would cover only the north of the "Midlands" area. We have hopes in time of engaging Trevor, or some other expert, for a book on the southern part of the area, but this is a start.

The Author

TREVOR FISHER is 49 years old. He graduated in History and Politics from Warwick University and now teaches History at Newcastle under Lyme College. He has written several books on social history of which the latest is *Scandal; the Sexual Politics of Late Victorian Britain*, published in 1995.

Contents

Introduction

This book is an introduction to some important historic houses in the northern part of the western midlands; a description and a tribute to some much loved buildings. The houses and the gardens and parks surrounding them are attracting increasing numbers of visitors, but why do they continue to attract such attention and respect?

Many old houses have fine architecture, rich furnishings and beautiful grounds. They are rewarding places to visit and they preserve part of our history and culture. These things are obvious and sufficient explanation for the public's interest, but perhaps there is something more.

You might have visited Birmingham's Aston Hall one autumn evening, when it was magically illuminated by thousands of candles. These events attract thousands, showing the fascination of Birmingham people with the great Jacobean house. It is a vast and extraordinary building, quite unlike any house that most of us have lived in. There are towering brick walls, scores of windows and cascades of pitched roofs bristle with amazing chimneys, there are towers topped with jolly pepper pots and insanely elaborate gables. What does it all mean? It is quite above and beyond the normal in scale, architecture, decoration and furnishings. This is not at all surprising, because that is exactly what its owner and designer intended; to put on a show you would never forget. These houses were demonstrations of great power and affluence which succeeded so well that they still dominate their localities.

Interest in Britain's historic houses and parks is widespread, but people wanting to enjoy this rich heritage do not always know what is available to them or how to reach it. This book meets the need by surveying historic houses and parks open to the public in the north-west midlands - principally central Staffordshire and Shropshire. Most books about historic houses cover a wide area, such as the whole of Britain, meaning that if you live in the Midlands eight tenths of their contents will be out of reach. In addition, they often concentrate on certain well known houses. This book deals comprehensively with a wide range of houses in a large but limited area.

Introductory chapters describe the development of the houses over the centuries, their architecture, gardens and parks. Then there is a section for each house or garden giving a history and description, with notes on facilities, such as a cafe or tea room, and how to get there by car or public transport (if any). I have given six figure map references to pinpoint locations. If you are not familiar with these you will find a simple explanation on the Ordnance Survey Landranger Maps. Note that, because bus services are subject to instant expansion, contraction or disappearance, we just give you the relevant County Council enquiry line. They can give details of all operators and services.

I have tried to avoid using technical and architectural terms so there are not many, but I could not do without them altogether. There is no space in this book for an adequate glossary, and there is no need, because you can have ample explanation from the books on architecture available from any library. At the end of this book is a Reading List noting all the works refered to in the text. From time to time I will mention "Pevsner", which means either the Shropshire or Staffordshire volume of his series *The Buildings of England*.

Aston Hall, Birmingham

The Historic House

The ancient counties of Shropshire and Staffordshire have a
wealth of fascinating historic houses, providing rich insights
into the lives of our ancestors. They were built over over five
centuries, from the late mediaeval Acton Burnell Castle, to the
nostalgic Victorian Arts and Crafts revivalism of Wightwick
Manor. The period between the building of these two provided a
remarkable range of houses and parks, each offering a unique
glimpse of life in the past, from the age of the castle to the
age of electricity.

Notable houses have been built at all periods from the Roman
Conquest to the present, but convention refers to "historic"
houses and gardens as those built between the end of the middle
ages and World War I. This was the period when Britain was
ruled by aristocrats and landed gentry, living for the most part
in the country and off the rents from the land they owned. Town
houses did exist of course, but even when a family made money
living in a town as merchants or bankers, land was the only secure
basis of wealth. They sought land and a house as an investment.

Great houses and their gardens have their roots in the life of the
aristocracy and the landed gentry, but they are quite distinct from
the military dwelling of classic feudalism, the castle. The wealthy
and powerful lived behind these ugly but formidable walls because
of the violence of mediaeval society, which continued until the end
of the Wars of the Roses in 1485, with echoes well into the Tudor
period that followed.

Castles, for my purposes, are outside the pale. Where a castle is
named, readers will usually find a house has been built where a
castle once stood. Splendid though castles might be, they are dealt
with elsewhere. This book is about historic houses, that is, houses
which were not just "machines for living in", as a modern architect
put it, but buildings designed to display wealth and power.

As the castle had ceased to be a desirable or necessary residence
after the feudal period, the powerful sought to display their power
and secure their position by a display of wealth and culture. Prof-
essor Mark Girouard put it in a nutshell by writing of the great
houses; *[Life in the English Country House.]*

"Essentially they were power houses - the houses of a ruling class...This power was based on the ownership of land...The point of land was the tenants and rent which came with it. A landowner could call on his tenants to fight for him, in the early days, and to vote for him, or his candidate, in its later days... Anyone who had sufficient resources and followers, and displayed them with enough prominence, was likely to be offered jobs and perquisites by the central government in return for his support."

This did not mean that the owners of great houses did not value splendour and beauty for their own sake; many did. But anyone who followed their cultural and aesthestic tastes without an eye for political and economic reality soon found that their houses became a major liability. Every landowner knew of families ruined by extravagance, and some cautionary tales appear in this book. The point of the expense of a fine house was to use it to maintain fortune and position.

Conspicuous consumption was the prerogative of the rich. Lesser gentry and tenant farmers could not afford such extravagance. Nevertheless, they too needed to maintain their status in a society where social relations between master and servant could often be fraught. Some of the smaller houses in this book show a real attempt to assert dominance through architecture, notably the curious central tower at the Oak House, West Bromwich. However the real interest of smaller houses like Blakesley Hall and Ford Green Hall is in the hints they give in the relationship of master and servants in houses which were too small to have a backstairs and tradesmans' entrance. They were little more than glorified farm houses, but the fact that they were called "hall" shows the social pretension and the real exertion of power and ambition which lay behind the buildings and their owners.

This use of houses as social and economic weapons continued only so long as land sustained the ruling class, and that ended as industrial and commercial wealth grew during the 19th century. The dominance of land was long in dying. Even as late as the 1870's more wealth lay in land than in industry or commerce, but the agricultural depression at the end of Victoria's reign delivered the coup de grace, and the whole way of life came to an end after World War I. The world of *Upstairs, Downstairs* vanished forever, but it left a legacy of five hundred years of conspicuous wealth and display, which at its best constitutes a rich legacy of art and culture. This area has as fine a heritage as most others, and through it we can trace the outline of a way of life which once dominated the whole country.

Five Centuries of Evolution

Houses have existed since ancient times, but those we call "historic" in England are the product of England's historical evolution since the late middle ages. Few houses built before the Norman conquest in 1066 exist. Even after the Conquest, for at least two centuries, houses hardly figured because the Normans had to live in castles. England was an occupied country, and the Norman French held down the Saxon peasantry by force. Their dwellings were military bases designed to provide security against rebellion. The Saxons, meanwhile, lived in wattle and daub huts which have not survived.

So in Norman society the wealthy lived in structures designed to resist armed attack, which had at the same time to be dwellings. The castle has been defined by M W Thompson *[The Decline of the Castle.]* as

> "a fortified residence in which the fortification predominates over the domestic aspect of the structure".

The great age of the castle in England was over by about 1400. Changes in warfare and growth of a powerful state much reduced the prospect of a serious rebellion requiring rich individuals to defend their property with a private army.

By the middle 13th century conditions had changed sufficiently for houses to begin to develop. The Norman ruling class had assimilated, becoming English speakers. Trade stimulated the growth of towns such as Stafford and Shrewsbury. Even so, English society remained very very violent, and castles continued to be built to the end of the 14th century.

They were still in use as late as the Civil War. The music hall song about ruins "that Cromwell knocked about a bit" reflects the difficulty that the New Model Army had in subduing Royalist castles. [Though the song may also have alluded to the results of the female singer's patronage of a pub called The Cromwell.] When parliament had won, it set about slighting, or wrecking, the remaining castles so they could never be used again.

But for a growing middle class and some of the aristocracy, houses had long been an attractive alternative, even if they had to be fortified. Very few houses remain from the 13th and early 14th centuries, but clearly their design was shaped by the persistent violence of mediaeval society. Conflict was always present, and security was only available from the protection of armed fighting men. This was the basis of feudalism, that is, of the whole social, economic and legal structure of society. The peasantry looked to the local knight for protection against lawlessness. The knight pledged allegience to an overlord, who in turn pledged allegience to the King to serve in large scale and international conflicts. In the other direction, the King granted tenancies of land to the major lords who leased it to lesser ones, who in turn leased portions to the local knights and so on. The rents were paid in produce or agricultural and military service. The means of subsistence was tied to the means of protection, and at all levels the bearing of arms was crucial.

A local example of the lawlessness and violence of the time was the bloody fight on the road between the Staffordshire hamlets of Mavesyn Ridware and Handsacre in 1403. Sir Robert Maveysn and Sir William Handsacre rode out of their respective fortified houses to join the impending battle of Shrewsbury. Mavesyn supported Henry IV, Handsacre backed Harry Hotspur. They met in open country and immediately fought their own private battle. Mavesyn killed Handsacre and went on to Shrewsbury, where he was himself killed. According to local legend, Mavesyn is a corruption of the Norman French "mal-voisins" - dangerous neighbour. Whatever the truth of that, dangerous neighbours abounded in England, and the only security lay in belonging to or commanding an armed band.

Obviously the houses which have survived are those of people rich enough to command such a band, and rich enough too, to build in relatively long lasting materials - timber, brick or stone. Thus historic housing in England from its very earliest days was the housing of powerful people. And a house was not just a dwelling for those who aspired to wealth and power, it was one of the key levers for gaining and maintaining both. Its role was particularly clear in the middle ages.

The knight or lord was only as powerful as the armed support he could command, and he sought to surround himself with armed ret-ainers. Thus the centre of the mediaeval house was the Great Hall, a room big enough to contain the whole of the knight's household for meals. Eating together was essential to maintain loyalty, with the seating arrangements organised in strict heirarchy. After the meal, entertainment was provided by minstrels. In a large house they would play in a separate gallery overlooking the Hall. Genuine examples have not survived in this area, but a good example of a re-creation can be found at Wightwick Manor, near Wolverhampton. But by the mid 14th century the Great Hall was in decline. William Langland commented in 1362:

> "Wretched is the hall ... each day in the week
> There the Lord and Lady liketh not to sit,
> Now have the rich a rule to eat by themselves
> In a privy chamber ..."

Piers Ploughman

Outside, the mediaeval house would have at least some defensive features, at the least a moat. The number of Moat House pubs in the country owes more to the strength of folk memory than actual survivals, but the Moat House at Acton Trussell, on the Stafford side of M6 Junction 13, is one example of a real mediaeval moated house, albeit much rebuilt. The remains of moats are also visible at the Moat House in Longnor near Shrewsbury, and strikingly at Upton Cresset near Bridgnorth.

The houses, more precisely huts, of the peasants would huddle by the house of the knight/lord for protection. Thus the plan of the English village was formed in the later middle ages. In towns, the same need for protection was supplied by town walls with fortified gates that would be closed at night or when attacked. Remains of these can be seen in Shrewsbury and Bridgnorth, and an echo can be heard in the names of streets in Stafford, such as North Walls and Eastgate Street. With the decline of violence in the Tudor period the rich could and did abandon defence for display.

The classic English mansion, in its heyday from the Tudor to the Regency period, went through several recognisable styles. As I have said, their builders wished to demonstrate their power, wealth and above all their culture. To show how cultured they were, it was desirable to follow the latest fashion in building, so as far as possible they employed the most up to date designers and architects. This is true even of a building like the late 17th century Sudbury Hall. Although it was designed by the owner, George Vernon, who was not a professional architect, he went to great pains to use the latest ideas and the best designers he could afford.

The importance of style in the building of the great houses and parks is undeniable. However, following fashion was not as rigid as some text books suggest. Fashion always took time to spread across the country, and older styles persisted long after the first examples of a newer one had emerged. The neo-classical Palladian revival, for example, began with Inigo Jones' Queen's House at Greenwich in 1616, but it only really became popular in the early 18th century, after the Baroque style of the late 17th century had past its heyday. Similarly in landscape, Tom Williamson *[Polite Landscapes]* has argued that the old style of rigid, formal gardens survived well into the 18th century, rather than disappearing with the rise of the neo-classical, Palladian house.

Queens House, Greenwich

Architects in the modern sense did not exist until the impact of the Renaissance in Elizabethan England, which is illustrated by Moreton Corbet Castle near Shrewsbury. Even after architects emerged as a recognised profession, they worked mostly under the close supervision of their patrons, so much of the amateur tradition of vernacular architecture survived into the 19th century. When the professional architect in the modern sense finally emerged in the Victorian period, the development marked the collapse of style as a coherent guide to the age of a building. Architects were trained in all styles and in none, and used them eclectically as they and their patrons desired. Until the Victorian period however, styles went through a series of developments.

Vernacular Style

Until the Tudor period, most houses in England were not designed by a known individual, but followed rules of thumb developed by builders over the centuries, through trial and error. Builders had learnt by experience what local materials were usable, and what methods could survive the rigours of the English climate. Stone buildings followed the methods perfected by the masons who built the mediaeval cathedrals and castles. Acton Burnell Castle illustrates this clearly. Stone built houses were, however, few and far between until the Elizabethan period. Most were timber framed with wattle and daub walls, expensive brick or stone being reseved for chimneys, which had to be fireproof.

Timber framing in its earliest mediaeval form was the "cruck" type. A naturally curved tree trunk was split and the two halves set opposite each other to form an arch. Across two or more arches was placed a ridge pole, to form a structure like a tent. From this primitive method developed the more ambitious post and truss timber framed houses built from the 15th to the early 17th century. These had rectangular box-like frames supporting a row of triangular roof trusses which were tied together with a longitudinal ridge board and purlins. Because several such units could be jointed together using a variety of pieces of timber, houses could become quite large, as in the Oak House, West Bromwich, and Ancient High House in Stafford.

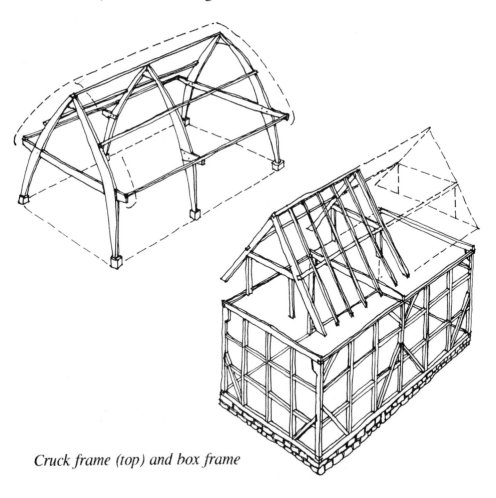

Cruck frame (top) and box frame

The Tudor Period

After the battle of Bosworth ended the wars of the Roses in 1485, England developed a strong central state under the Tudors which ended the most violent disorder. The ensuing peace enabled the rich to devote more time and resources to developing house design. They also became aware of continental influences and the Renaissance, which had started in Italy around 1350 and spread across Europe. Britain was a relative backwater, so it was not until the Stuarts two centuries later that English architecture was much influenced by Continental developments. In the meantime it remained vernacular, albeit with Renaissance trimmings.

This period saw the timber framed house develop its highest form, giving us the splendid example of the Stafford High House, built in 1595, and many fine houses in Shrewsbury, notably the Abbots House. Timber framed houses continued to be built into the seventeenth century, and proved suprisingly durable. Other examples are the Oak House in West Bromwich, Blakesley Hall, Birmingham, and Ford Green Hall in Stoke on Trent.

However splendid timbering might be, the advantages of stone and brick were overwhelming, and growing wealth in the Tudor period meant that these materials, especially brick, were increasingly preferred to timber framing and wattle and daub inserts. The architecture reflected that this was a period of transition between the late mediaeval Perpendicular Gothic style and the continental influences of the Renaissance. Good examples of Tudor stone buildings survive in Wilderhope Manor, Weston Hall, Shipstone, Benthall and the splendid ruin of Moreton Corbet Castle, which was cannibalised from a genuine castle on the site. A partial change was for the panels of later timber framed houses to be infilled with brick. This was cheaper than a completely brick or stone building and very common in the Midlands. On other sites, timber framed Tudor buildings were later clad in stone or brick walls - as with Whitmore Hall.

Typical Tudor country houses were of two types - either the old quadrangle plan with a gatehouse, or the newer type of rectangular block with short projecting wings and often a projecting porch. This formed the E shape which coincided so nicely with the reign of Elizabeth I. There was greater tendency to symmetry than in the preceding period, showing some awareness of the Renaissance.

The interior arrangements remain mediaeval, at least in the earlier Tudor houses, with the basic arrangement of a Great Hall with service rooms at one end and private rooms at the other. However "State" rooms begin to appear, like the Great Chamber and the Dining Chamber.

Whatever form of building was chosen, substantial houses remained power houses. By this period, power was no longer a question of armed force, but maintained by a display of wealth, culture and sophistication. Characteristic of the new Tudor love of display were elaborate gatehouses. These had been a frequent feature of mediaeval houses and often formed the entrance to a courtyard as in the fine example at Maevysn Ridware. The Tudor period produced splendid free standing structures which were as much status symbols as functional entrances. A fine brick gatehouse stands at Upton Cressett, while an even finer stone example is the Tixall Gatehouse, east of Stafford.

Externally designs remain mediaeval - square headed windows with mullions and transoms, and sharply pitched roofs with triangular gables. Brick became more widely used, and bay and oriel windows more common. Tall, elaborate and ornamental chimneys, as with the "barleysugar" twisted design appear, testifying to the increased use of coal as fuel, and the desire to make a functional feature attractive. Good examples are Weston Hall near Stafford,

Tixall Gatehouse, near Stafford

Wilderhope Manor, Benthall Hall, and Shipton Hall in Shropshire. Internally there are wall fireplaces with rich overmantels, linen-fold panels and relief plasterwork, such as the rich ceilings at Wilderhope, Upton Cresset Gatehouse, and Morville Hall in Shropshire.

These are among the last examples of a truly vernacular achitecture. By the end of the Tudor period in the late 16th century continental influences begun to dominate, and can be seen in Moreton Corbet castle, "by far the most important surviving Elizabethan house in Shropshire" according to Pevsner *[Buildings of England - Shropshire]* which he relates to Longleat. He calls it a facade articulated "in the French way" by attached Tuscan columns below and Ionic columns above, with slim ogee gables.

By the time Elizabeth I died in 1603, Renaissance and continental influences were flowing freely into England. Her long reign of 45 years had given stability to an increasingly wealthy gentry and artistocracy, who employed their new opportunities in an astonishing burst of house building. Late Gothic and early Tudor styles were now blended with the French Renaissance style of the Loire valley chateaux, and decoration from the Low Countries and Germany, with Flemish strapwork and Dutch gables taken from style books - a new form of communication. The best example of this is the ruin of Moreton Corbet castle, though Aston Hall, a Jacobean development of Elizabethan trends, shows the process taken a step further.

The Stuarts and the Neo-Classical Revival

There appears no objective reason why the accession of James I in 1603 should have marked changes in architecture, but his arrival from Scotland did coincide with a new approach.

The houses of the early Stuart period, the reigns of James I and Charles I, are essentially developments from the Tudor period. They continued to emphasise symmetry without yet much interest in pure classic form. The so called Jacobean style was a development from the great houses of late Tudor England. A florid mixture of archictectural features was applied to the characteristic E Plan houses of the period. So the entrance and porch might be under a semicircular arch flanked by squat classical columns that no Greek would have known. Above might be an ornamental panel featuring heraldry framed by stone scrolls, all topped by further storeys of elaborately carved flummery between further columns of different designs. Great fun. Sudbury is good example though it only reaches two storeys; see our front cover. Another specimen is Aston Hall - though a pretty restrained one. It was built by Sir Thomas Holte from 1618 to 1635, but even during construction it was stylistically overtaken by the latest London fashion.

In 1615 a brilliant designer of court masques was appointed Surveyor of the King's works by James I. Inigo Jones had been taken to Italy on the Grand Tour by the Earl of Arundel, and was perhaps the first English architect to see Classical Roman buildings in situ. He came back determined to base his buildings on true Classical models, and in so doing sowed the seeds of neo-classicism in British architecture. His Queen's House at Greenwich (1616) was the first true neo-classical house in Britain.

The influence of Inigo Jones and the early neo-classic revival is hard to detect outside London. The smaller houses continued in the Elizabethan manner - small stone houses in Tudor vernacular, and timber framed houses for the wealthier yeomanry and professional classes. The latter reached their peak in the late Elizabethan and Jacobean periods, with more widely spaced timber struts reflecting growing confidence in building techniques, but counterbalanced by use of wooden struts to make complex ornamental patterns in the walls. These are not structural elements, but purely decorative.

Inside the houses, the strict *Upstairs, Downstairs* pattern of rigid demarcation between the servants quarters and those of the wealthy employers was established well before the 18th century. The need for a tightly knit household geared to fighting for the lord had long disappeared, and with it the need for the Lord to associate daily with the men he might have to lead into battle. Accordingly the Lord and his family moved out of the Hall for meals, in most great houses by the mid-15th century, leaving it as the servants' dining room.

By the early 16th century architects provided separate servants' sleeping quarters, well away from those of the owners and with a separate stairway at the back of the house. Backstairs were being built in the early 16th century, and the new arrangements can be seen at Aston Hall. The grand staircase for the gentry stands on the south side of the house. A mean servants' stair stands on the north side, mirroring the grand staircase and linking the servants' sleeping quarters in the attic with the kitchen. By the middle 17th century, the servants were moved from the Great Hall, which became an entrance hall with the grand staircase placed within it. Girouard sees this as taking place first at Coleshill, Berkshire, about 1650, when the architect Roger Pratt put the servants into a hall in the basement.

The great houses of England were starting to obey the rule set down by Roger Pratt in 1660, namely that a house should be "so contrived...that the ordinary servants may never publicly appear in passing to and from for their occasions there". Thus by the middle 17th century *Upstairs, Downstairs* had arrived and the rigid class divisions it symbolised continued well into the twentieth century.

In the history of architecture, the 17th century is dominated by two giants - Inigo Jones in the first half of the century, and Christpher Wren in the second. Jones brought about the classical revival, Wren invented English Baroque. But neo-classicism did not become an established style in the 17th century. Architecture associated with the court was not ideally suited to a country slipping towards Civil War, and even after the restoration in 1660 strict classicism did not become dominant. The work of Wren and the Baroque school dominated great building works till the early 18th century. The influence of classicism can be seen locally in the great houses of the Restoration period, Sudbury and Weston Park. Sudbury Hall, built by George Vernon from 1659 to 1701, and Weston Hall, started in 1671, were both the work of owners acting as their own architects and hiring experts as the mood took them. Weston Hall was built by Lady Wilbraham, one of the few women to create a great house.

By the end of the 17th century a concern for symmetry, clean lines and the use of classical decoration took hold in the smaller scale houses of the gentry. The "Queen Anne" house developed as early as the 1680s. Essentially a box with a hipped roof and classical decoration, it was invented by the Dutch and rapidly spread across England. Curiously, it was not particularly popular in the West Midlands, though the re-shaped Whitmore Hall near Newcastle under Lyme is a good example.

Nor was the English Baroque style invented by Wren particularly popular in an area which was relatively poor in the late 17th and early 18th centuries. The Baroque style was a theatrical approach to architecture, relying on huge buildings carrying an enormous weight of detail thrown together with flamboyant decoration. The results, as in Hawksmoor's churches, Vanbrugh's Castle Howard and Blenheim Palace, are grandiose. Because they were designed for theatrical effect rather than domestic utility, they were enormously expensive to build and maintain.

There is little Baroque architecture in the West Midlands area, though the small church by Ingestre Hall east of Stafford is said to have been designed by Wren. Baroque architecture made far less impact than its successor, neo-classicism, and by the early 18th century there was a reaction in favour of Inigo Jones and classical simplicity.

The Classical Era

By the time the Hanoverians came to the throne in the person of George I in 1714, English architecture had discovered the formalism of classical Rome, while English gardens had discovered naturalism. The change of direction in gardening is dramatic. In the Elizabethan and Stuart periods, gardens and landscaping had been rigid and rule bound; dominated by paths running in dead straight lines as if to emphasis the domination of nature by man. But in the 18th century, under the influence of gardeners like William Kent, Lancelot "Capability" Brown and Humphrey Repton, formal gardens were ripped up and replaced by carefully planned picturesque landscapes artfully designed to look natural. Brown worked at Himley Hall, Trentham Gardens, Chillington and Weston, Repton at Attingham near Shrewsbury. English Parkland aspired to be a version of the idealised Roman landscapes found in the paintings of Claude and Poussin. Apparently natural arrangments of hills, valleys, rivers, lakes, trees and shrubs were contrived with immense labour and expense, and dotted with a romantic sprinking of mausoleums, classical bridges, ancient temples and roman statues.

The finest local example is Shugborough. Admiral Anson made a fortune by circling the globe in the mid 18th century, and put his money into the family estate. The wealth and power of the magnates who followed this fashion was such that, if a local village was inconveniently placed in the landscape, it could be swept away and rebuilt elsewhere. Shugborough is one example of just such a process.

The Ansons combined a taste for picturesque landscape with an interest in Chinese and Classical Greek architecture. The former was applied to a pagoda. The Greek appears in parkland strewn with little temples and fanciful monuments, with romantic names like the Temple of the Winds and Arch of Hadrian. As the 18th century Grand Tour developed, James

"Athenian" Stuart and Nicholas Revett visited Athens and drew the monuments. Stuart then made a career of erecting copies in English parks, and Shugborough shows his work at its best. The architecture of the English country house in the mid-18th century was much influenced by a return to the ideas of the 16th century Italian architect, Palladio. Palladio had himself been influenced by the Ancient Roman architect Vitruvius, and the hallmarks of his approach were a concern for restraint and order, symmetry and the keeping of rules - the rules laid down by Vitruvius. There is no doubt that in England this movement was a reaction to the Baroque, which had seemed to be getting out of hand. Architects adopting Palladianism could produce splendid facades, notably when the formula of a central block with a classical portico and flanking pavilions is employed by an architect of genius, as James Paine proved at Kedlestone in Derbyshire.

Palladianism was dominant in the late 18th century, but restless spirits increasingly challenged what they thought aloof and hide - bound. Indeed, even at the height of the neo-classical period, are there early hints of rebellion in those parks and follies? Why is there such a contrast between that constipated great house at Shugborough and those airy temples. They are classical enough in design, yet the concept was totally romantic. As early as the 1750s Horace Walpole began a fashion for reviving Gothic architecture with his house at Strawberry Hill. Bold spirits penetrated beyond Rome to look at the Greek springs of Roman architecture, in what was then a bandit ridden Greek peninsula. Travellers to China brought back designs for pagodas, and the British conquest of India in the 18th century brought them into contact with the Mogul architecture. Successful architects became adept in many styles. The towering genius of the Regency period, John Nash, built Gothic houses, cottages ornee, neo-classical terraces around Regents Park, the Royal Pavilion at Brighton in the style of a Moghul palace, and Cronkhill house on the Attingham Park Estate in an Italian style. Cronkhill directly inspired the now demolished ducal house at Trentham Gardens designed by Sir Charles Barry, and a thousand imitators. With Nash (1752 - 1835) architectural history entered the age of the all purpose architect, who was adept at all styles of building but could no longer claim to express the spirit of an age in the way that Elizabethan architecture, the Jacobeans, the baroque style, and the Palladians had done.

Romantics and Victorians

In the late 18th century this siren call of the exotic coalesced
into a challenge to the cool rationalism of the Enlightenment
in the form of the Romantic Movement. This is as obvious in
the painting, poetry and music of the period as in the architecture. Romanticism valued the emotional against the rational,
feelings against ideas. In architecture this led to a revolt from
neo-classicism and its concern with rule dominated, symmetry.
It prompted a return to Gothic style, copying haphazard, mediaeval development which had grown over centuries.

The finest example of the style in this area is the estate of the
Earl of Shrewsbury at Alton, in Staffordshire. The work at Alton
Towers by the 15th Earl was developed by the 16th Earl between
1831 and 1840 into one of the finest buildings of the Romantic
movement in Britain. The grounds are now best known as our
largest theme park, but the house deserves recognition for its
connection with the Gothic revival. Pugin also tried to build a
romantic mock castle on the side of the Churnet valley.

The last attempt at a coherent stylistic approach to building
was the Gothic revival of the mid 19th century, before Victorian
architecture collapsed into tastelessness. Gothic architecture as
revived by Walpole produced a plethora of mock cathedrals and
mock castles which owed more to the romantic dreams of rich
eccentrics like Walpole and William Beckford than to the mediaeval. A W N Pugin (1812-52) launched a crusade for a return to
genuine Gothic styles, covering Barry's Houses of Parliament
design of 1836 with a Perpendicular facade. Pugin showed that
the styles of Gothic architecture could be applied to Victorian
houses, though at Alton Towers he was too late to save a start-
lingly eclectic design, and Alton is a curious fairy tale Gothic
building.

Pugin began a "battle of the styles" between classical and Gothic
which continued throughout the 19th century. It was a mock battle.
Most architects, like Nash, simply used whatever style their patrons
desired. Once the idea of recycling the architecture of the middle
ages had become established in the early years of the century, architects came to realise that any style could be used at will. By the
time Victoria came to the throne in 1837, architects had ceased
trying to develop a consistent style for their period. They raided

the history books and built mock castles, mock abbeys, mock cathedrals, mock timber framing, mock Elizabethan, mock Stuart, mock neo-classical, mock Italian, mock Mogul Indian, or whatever took their or their clients fancy.

The new middle class made wealthy by the industrial revolution mostly lived in towns, and if they used their new money to buy country estates - as did Richard Arkwright, the first cotton magnate, they chose their styles from a style book. "Tudorbeathan" became a dominant style, immortalised in millions of semi detached houses as the suburbs sprawled out from the towns.

The eclectic approach of the 19th century can be seen in several houses covered by this book. The finest example was Barry's Italianate Trentham Gardens House for the Duke of Sutherland, demolished in 1912. However the stable block still exists and gives an insight into what he designed. The top of the tower was removed to Sandon Hall, where it survives, appallingly neglected. Sandon Hall itself is an example of mid-Victorian architecture, having been rebuilt after a fire in June 1848. The The architect, William Burn, chose the Jacobean style, and worked it to provide a reasonably harmonious design. The same cannot be said of another major house of the period in Staffordshire, Keele Hall. This was rebuilt for the Sneyd family by Anthony Salvin, in an odd mix of Elizabethan and Jacobean.

However, an eclectic approach did not have to be a mish-mash, as is shown by Wightwick Manor near Wolverhampton. This was built at the end of the 19th century by the Mander paint family in the style of a mock mediaeval manor house, using the ideas of the Arts and Crafts movement pioneered by William Morris. This was a development from the Romantic movement, but it looked to the past not of the great mediaeval churches and religion, which had at least happened, but of an imagined golden age of yeomen and craftsmen. It was deeply pessimistic and nostalgic, but the positive consequences of the movement were wallpapers, fabrics, ceramics, wrought ironwork and building in some of the most enduringly attractive domestic art of any period. At Wightwick Manor the mixture of brickwork, hung tiles and half timbering is suprisingly effective and the entire atmosphere of this richly furnished and decorated house is harmonious and comfortable.

The houses described in this book all required a force of low paid servants, and the social and economic conditions which supplied them reached their apogee before World War I. That war ended the era of cheap labour, and the invention of electric labour saving gadgets transformed life in the home. Houses designed to accomodate a large number of people, either to fight or to service the house or both, were out of date. From 1937 The National Trust was allowed to take houses into its care in place of death duties, and so they became official museum pieces by Act of Paliament.

Great houses continued, and continue, to be built, but the era of what Mark Girouard calls power houses had come to an end. In the age of democratic mass communications, those aspiring to power did not need houses to overawe or impress supporters or voters. Even if they did, the servant class had gone to other work. Thus after five centuries, the history of the house turned away from the display of wealth and learning, leaving behind a rich heritage we can still enjoy to-day.

Speedwell Castle, Brewood, Staffs;
one of few local examples of
Strawberry Hill Gothic

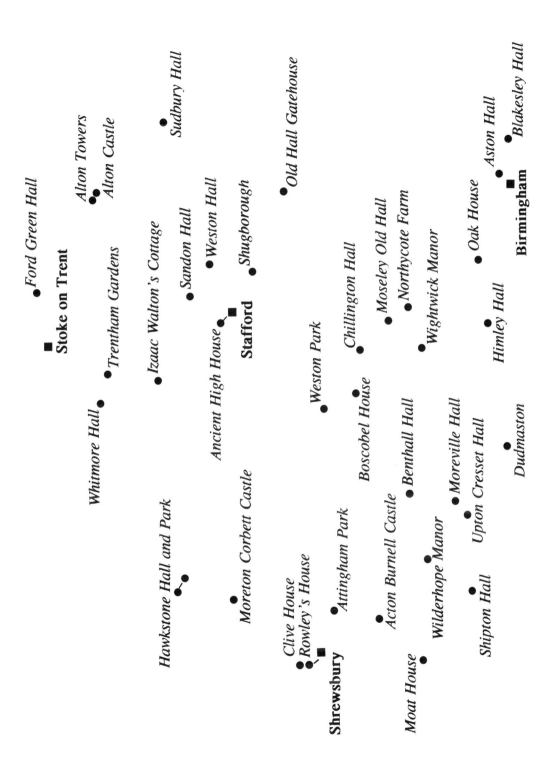

Ford Green Hall

Stoke on Trent

Alton Towers
Alton Castle

Sudbury Hall

Old Hall Gatehouse

Blakesley Hall

Aston Hall

Birmingham

Trentham Gardens

Izaac Walton's Cottage

Sandon Hall

Weston Hall

Shugborough

Moseley Old Hall

Northycote Farm

Oak House

Whitmore Hall

Ancient High House

Stafford

Chillington Hall

Wightwick Manor

Himley Hall

Weston Park

Boscobel House

Hawkstone Hall and Park

Moreton Corbett Castle

Benthall Hall

Moreville Hall

Dudmaston

Clive House
Rowley's House

Attingham Park

Acton Burnell Castle

Upton Cresset Hall

Wilderhope Manor

Shrewsbury

Shipton Hall

Moat House

(20)

Acton Burnell Castle

WHERE
Map reference SJ 534018; 6 miles south of Shrewsbury and 5
miles west of Much Wenlock. Signposted from Acton Burnell.

TRANSPORT
No public transport.

ACCESS & FACILITIES
Owned by English Heritage and open all reasonable hours.
There is no charge, nor any facilities or guidebook. It
makes a fine, grassy place for a picnic.

HISTORY
The ruined building at Acton Burnell in Shropshire is neither a
conventional stately home nor a castle. It is a most interesting
survival of that period in the late middle ages when England's
rulers began to move away from fortified residences to genuine
stone houses. As the only stone architecture to hand was that of
castles or churches, and churches were hardly a model for domestic architecture, it is not surprising that the house looks
superficially like a castle or fortified manor house.

The "Castle" was built by Robert Burnell, chaplain and secretary to Prince Edward. Burnell became one of the most powerful
men in England when the Prince became King Edward I in 1272
and he was made Lord Chancellor and Bishop of Bath and Wells.
At Bath he built the sumptuous Hall and Chapel of the Bishops'
Palace. Acton Burnell was his family home, and in 1284 he obtained a Royal license to crenellate (that is - fortify) a house in
the village. The present building was erected at some time
between that date and the Bishop's death in 1293.

Despite the license to crenellate, the building could never have
been a castle. The large ground floor windows would have
been easy to attack, there are three doorways, no moat and no
evidence of a defensive wall. At best, this was a fortified house
similar to Stokesay a few miles south, or the tower houses of the
14th and 15th centuries.

DESCRIPTION
In plan the building is a rectangle 75 feet by 54 feet, looking like
the keep of a mediaeval castle, and with towers at each corner.

Roofing seems to have been by two parallel gables behind the battlements, but the roof fell in centuries ago. The towers were capped during the romantic revival of the 18th century.

Pevsner argues that the architectural detail is more refined than at Stokesay, but the house gives an impression of crudity. Even for the rich and powerful, life in the middle ages must have been cold, draughty and uncomfortable. There are no large fireplaces or chimneys. Garderobes, or lavatory shafts reaching from upper storey to basement and cleared out by hand, were provided in the north-west tower and the west projection between the towers. The style of the house is largely that of the stone keep of a castle. The ground floor is an undercroft, with the main rooms lying above. The eastern two thirds contained hall and solar, or living room, while the western third dispensed with the undercroft and contained three floors of rooms, probably offices and bedrooms.

There are many unanswered questions about this house. Nothing can be seen of a staircase from the undercroft to the main floor, though one must have existed. A spiral staircase ran up from the main floor to the second floor in the south-west tower. Historians cannot locate precisely the Chapel, which Bishop Burnell would certainly have had, or the kitchen. Given the importance of Robert Burnell in the court of Edward 1, the house shows the difficulties that historians have in researching mediaeval history.

Even the site of the Parliament of 1284, which produced an Act called the "Statute of Acton Burnell", is obscure. The house would not have been large enough to accommodate a Parliament. It is likely that the extremely long building to the West of the house was the site. It was probably a barn, but at 157 feet long and 40 feet wide it was very large. Only the gable ends remain, but even these are impressive. Was the barn built for the Parliament? Pevsner suggests this was the first Parliament in English History at which the Commons were properly represented.

The later history of the house is obscure. A Sir Nicholas Burnell is commemorated in the nearby church as having died in 1382. Thereafter the family seems to have died out and a Lees family become the local squires. Acton Burnell Hall is a fine Georgian House which is now a school, it was built in 1811 and by then the "castle" had long since become a romantic ruin appealing to the picturesque taste of the 18th century.

Acton Burnell Castle, Shropshire

Alton Castle and Alton Towers

WHERE
Map references SK SK 073425 (Castle) and SK 073435 (Towers);
12 miles east of Stoke on Trent. Alton Towers and its grounds
are the famous theme park; the Castle stands in the village of Alton
on the opposite (south) bank of the River Churnet. This is just off
the B5032 between Cheadle and Rocester.

TRANSPORT
Buses run - phone 01785 223344; masses of car space.

ACCESS & FACILITIES
Alton Towers is owned by Madame Tussauds; for details of opening
times and charges phone 01538 703344. Access to the buildings and
garden cannot be separated from the theme park, unless by special
arrangement. Eating and other facilities are excellent.

Alton Castle is owned by the Monumental Trust who will open it
to the public when repair work is complete. To find the present
position and details of opening hours etc phone 01538 703300.

THE CASTLE
The present Alton Castle is mock Gothic and built on the ruins of
the mediaeval castle of Bertram de Verdun. Pugin, the great early
Victorian architect responsible for the exterior of the Houses of
Parliament, designed the building for the 16th Earl of Shrewsbury
in the 1840s. Work started in 1844 and was not finished in 1852
when Pugin died. It is a curious design for a castle, looking even
less like a mediaeval English castle than nearby Alton Towers.
There is a distinct resemblance to the ad hoc jumble of designs
found in the early Gothic revival, and castigated by Pugin
himself in *The Principles of Pointed Architecture*.

The Castle may not be authentic, but it is certainly romantic on
its wooded crag above the River Churnet, looking like a Rhineland
Schloss. Until recently it was owned by a Catholic order and closed
to the public, but is now being restored by the Monumental Trust
directed by the Conservationist, Stephen Weeks. The Castle will
feature a "Candlelight Tour" and a "Wars of the Roses Feast".
Guest suites will be furnished as country house bedrooms and
Pugin's chapel will be used to solemnize marriages. The whole
castle will become a late 20th century leisure facility but
retain its historical ambience. That's showbiz.

Alton Castle

ALTON TOWERS

Alton Towers is Britain's largest theme park, visited by thousands
of children and their parents each day. Yet at the heart of the park
is one of the largest ruins of the Gothic revival in Britain, set in
one of the most splendid gardens of the early 19th century. The
development of Alton Towers as a leisure playground has overshadowed both the ruin and the garden. Since the park was taken
over by Madame Tussaud's there are signs that the importance
of the grounds and buildings will be recognised.

HISTORY

The origins of the settlement at Alton are lost in Saxon mist.
The earliest which can be proved is that of Bertram de Verdun,
who built the original Alton Castle half a mile south of the
present Towers early in the 12th century. It was destroyed in
the Civil War. In 1412 the estate passed into the hands of John
Talbot, 1st Earl of Shrewsbury, and then through the Shrewsbury family which acquired land over the centuries, until the
15th Earl inherited in 1787. He lived at Heythrop in Oxfordshire,
but after his marriage moved to Alton. The romantic remoteness
and wildness of the Churnet valley was certainly a factor drawing
the Earl, and it provided an ideal spot to build the fashionable
Gothic style mansion with an extensive garden.

From 1814 to 1827 the 15th Earl and his wife, both devout Roman Catholics, devoted much of his considerable fortune to converting the existing Alveton Lodge into the Gothic Alton Abbey, which is the core of the present house. However the 15th Earl is most famous for converting the Churnet Valley into a magnificent garden. There was no water on the slopes of the valley, and hence no trees and few plants, so water was brought from a spring two miles to the north. The Earl employed two gardeners, Thomas Allanson and Robert Abrahams, who were trained in the style of gardening employed at Stourhead and Stow and linked to the name of Capability Brown.

When Charles, 15th Earl of Shrewsbury, died in 1827 he was succeeded by his nephew John, also a Roman Catholic. John completed the garden, and after his mansion at Heythrop burned down in 1831 he decided to move permanently to Alton. The Abbey was renamed Alton Towers and expanded to befit the estate of England's premier Earl. By 1835 most of the work was finished, so it is not true to say that Pugin designed the Towers because he did not arrive at Alton until 1837. He did, however, decorate the Chapel and Banqueting Hall. He also built Alton Castle and St John's Hospital on the ruins of Bertram de Verdun's genuine castle in the village. The 16th Earl lavished money on entertaining and furnishing his house,

Alton Towers

so that when Queen Victoria visited it in 1832, on a journey which included Plas Newydd in Anglesey, Eaton Hall in Chester, and Chatsworth House in Derbyshire, Alton Towers was equal to them all.

Unlike the others, Alton Towers fell on hard times. After the death of the childless 17th Earl in 1856, the house was inherited by Earl Talbot of Ingestre, twenty miles to the south near Stafford. His inheritance was contested and the ensuing lawsuit bankrupted the estates. The contents had to be sold, and over 29 days in 1857 auctioneers emptied the Towers. To help pay for refurnishing, the new Earl opened the gardens to the public. This was very successful and special trains brought crowds of up to 30,000 people. The extra income helped to pay for the lavish lifestyle which the aristocracy enjoyed in the late 19th century. When the 20th Earl decided in 1896 to live apart from his wife, Alton Towers was neglected. He lived at Ingestre, she at Alton, and the Earl starved her of money. When the Countess took him to court, evidence was presented that the Towers was becoming derelict, and it never recovered. In 1924 the estate was sold to local businessmen who developed it for leisure purposes and had no interest in the house. The coup de grace was delivered by the Army, who occupied the Towers in World War Two and left it in such a state that when it was handed back in 1951, demolition of the interior was unavoidable.

DESCRIPTION.
Alton Towers itself is now only a shell, yet one of the most impressive ruins anywhere in the country. The facade is 450 feet long with a depth of 250 feet, making the house one of the largest in Britain. Seen across the lake through the trees, the Towers are impressively romantic. Close up, the impression is more of Gothic fantasy. Some parts of the house are modelled on mediaeval castles, looking like Warwick, others are a curious mixture of styles thrown together like a child's view of a mediaeval knight's residence. The Chapel, adjacent buildings and court yards are impressive Gothic reconstructions, but other sections, presumably added by the 16th Earl, are tacked on without any clear logic. To wander through the ruin is to marvel at the wealth of the Earls of Shrewsbury, if not at their taste.

The garden remains splendid. There are many fountains of which the most impressive is the 70 foot jet of the Pagoda fountain by the gardner Abrahams, copied from the To Ho pagoda in Canton. The inscription placed by the 16th Earl on the imitation Greek monument as a tribute to his uncle - *He Made The Desert Smile*, is entirely justified. Abrahams also designed the impressive conservatories, now restored to house palm trees and other oriental and exotic plants. Across the valley the Swiss Cottage commands a splendid view, and despite being turned into a restaurant, allows a visitor some insight into why, in the 19th century, the gardens could attract 30,000 visitors each day.

Ancient High House

WHERE
Greengate Street, Stafford. I expect you can find the town without directions.

TRANSPORT
There are bus and train services from all parts. Bus enquiries - 01785 223344. Leave your car at one of the many town centre car parks.

ACCESS & FACILITIES
Owned by Stafford District Council as a Tourist Information Centre. Open all year 9.00am to 5.00pm on Monday to Friday; 10.00am to 3.00pm Saturdays. Enquiries - 01785 40204. Nearby are dozens of pubs, cafes, tea shops and WCs.

HISTORY
The Ancient High House in the middle of Stafford's main Greengate Street is one of the most enigmatic houses in this book. Although said to be the largest timber framed town house in England, and the last major reminder of Stafford's old buildings, its history is largely unknown. It is exceptionally difficult to separate legend from fact and the current owners, Stafford District Council, have yet to bring out an accurate guidebook.

The house bears the date 1555, but Pevsner suggests that this is too early and the accepted date is 1595. 19th century sources suggest that either Richard or John Dorrington built the house, but although the Dorringtons were a prominent local family, they were not important enough to have left enough records to establish which one built the house. John Dorrington, Wool Merchant, is the most likely candidate. The Dorringtons seem to have held the house until 1733 when it was bought by a branch of Isaac Walton's family. But the legend that Walton himself owned it is untrue; he had been dead for fifty years. The legend that Charles I and Prince Rupert stayed in the house during the Civil War does seem to be true. The Mayor of Stafford, Mr Brooke Crutchley, is known to have owned the house in 1774 and to have divided it into two dwellings, the other part occupied by Samuel Twigg, Mercer. A drawing of 1823 shows a separate side entrance which supports the idea of internal subdivision. The house passed through a number of hands, including the prominent Staffordshire families of the Sneyds and Dyotts, but we have few details.

John Marson bought the house in 1826 and immediately converted it into shops. Modernising led to dangerous cutting away of structural members and mutilation of internal features. The house survived this, but by May 1972 deterioration had become serious, with corner

Ancient High House, Stafford

(29)

timbers rotting away from rain damage. Stafford Council had no wish to see a repeat of the demolition of other timber framed buildings, but realised that with the declining commercial value of the property, public ownership would be needed to save it. Prolonged negotiations led to the Council becoming owners in February 1981, and the house was saved.

DESCRIPTION
Ancient High House is a massive, four storeyed structure. The two storey porch and large mullioned windows are topped with four gables providing rooms in the roof space, and they create a most impressive facade, A pity the two shops flanking the porch wholly ruin the impression of age. The same is true of the side elevation on the alley running next to the intrusive MacDonalds' restaurant, where shops totally ruin the effect of the ancient timbering.

Inside, the rooms are a mish mash of office accomodation for the Council, half hearted attempts to provide exhibition space and some re-creation of the history of the house. The Staffordshire Yeomanry Museum has been added to the top floor, but on the whole the High House is disappointing. Stafford prides itself on being the town that found its castle. It is not yet the town that found its High House.

Aston Hall

WHERE
Map reference SP 078900; about 2 miles north of Birmingham City centre by the A38(M) and 1 mile south-west of Sphagetti Junction. The main entrance is on Trinity Road, Aston, Birmingham near Aston Villa Football Ground. The Hall is not well signposted; ask for "The Villa", and when you get there ask for the Hall.

TRANSPORT
Witton and Aston railway stations are nearby. There are frequent buses from the City Centre to Trinity Road and Church Road. Train and bus enquiries - 0121 200 2700. There is limited car parking space in the grounds; if need be use nearby streets.

ACCESS & FACILITIES
Aston Hall is owned by Birmingham City Council and normally open from March to November, but check details on 0121 327

0062 or 0121 235 2834. There is a small cafeteria and guide books are available. WCs are in the house. Entry is free.

HISTORY

Aston Hall is an exceptionally fine Jacobean Mansion which survives largely as it was built between 1618 and 1635. It stands, incongruous but proud, in a dreary part of inner city Birmingham. It was built by Sir Thomas Holte (1571 to 1654), 1st Baronet of his line, to celebrate his family becoming the dominant family of the area in the early 17th century. The Holtes had become increasingly important members of north Warwickshire society in the Tudor period, furnishing MPs, High Sheriffs and Deputy Lieutenants of the County. Their prosperity and status had grown to the point where Thomas Holte became a knight in 1603, and purchased the new title of baronet in 1611. Holte felt the family home at nearby Duddeston was beneath the dignity of his new position, and in 1618 began to build a new house on a ridge overlooking the Lichfield road.

Thomas Holte supported the King during the Civil War, and offered shelter to Charles I on the night of 18th October 1642 as he travelled to the Battle of Edgehill. The King's bedchamber was substantially altered in 1750 but still contains memorabilia of this visit. A shot fired from Parliamentary cannon in the seige of 1643 gouged a hole in the Great Stair, which has been deliberately left unrepaired to this day. Holte was then in his seventies and surrendered the house, which survived the rest of the war undamaged.

The Hall then passed out of history and became a backwater as Aston declined compared to its expansive neighbour, Birmingham. It was occupied by the Holte family until the death of the last Baronet, Sir Charles, in 1782. The family carried out sensitive remodelling in the 17th and 18th centuries, preserving the house's Jacobean character. The exterior is almost original, and even the interior was not substantially changed. Work was stopped after 1770 and the result is a "sleeping house", passed over by the Industrial Revolution and growth of the vast conurbation which swept over Aston in the 19th century.

The Hall survived by a series of fortunate accidents. After the death of Charles Holte, it passed by marriage to Abraham Bracebridge, who lost a fortune in industrial ventures and sold the Hall and park to speculators in 1817. The Manor of Aston was sold in 1818 but the Hall was let by James Watt jnr in 1819.

He was the son of the famous James Watt, partner of Birmingham's inventor, engineer and manufacturer, Matthew Boulton. Watt was attracted by the antiquity of the house, and made no major alterations apart from installing central heating. After Watt left in 1848 the owners made an unsuccessful attempt to turn house and park into an amusement park and went bankrupt in 1864. Birmingham Corporation bought the property, the first local authority in the country to buy a historic house.

DESCRIPTION

Aston Hall was built to the conventional compressed U-shape plan of the Jacobean period. Visitors enter directly into the Great Hall, descendant of the mediaeval Great Hall which was originally used both for dining and for business purposes. Sir Thomas's household had its meals in the Great Hall and tenants paid their rents here. The exceptionally fine Grand Staircase is markedly similar to that at the late Tudor Benthall Hall in Shropshire. It stands at one end of the Great Hall and rises through the house to reach the stately rooms of the Holtes and their guests. At the northern end of the house a more modest staircase gives access to the servants quarters in the attic, while a hazardous spiral staircase goes to the kitchens. The structure of the house fascinatingly mirrors its social divisions.

A particularly interesting feature of Aston Hall is the Long Gallery (136 feet, 44 metres long) running across the whole of the rear West Front of the house. Long galleries were a Tudor invention designed to give the owners of the house exercise in bad weather. But this is clearly a Jacobean house, one of the last to be completed before the Civil War, and the change in fashion brought about by Inigo Jones and the start of the classical revival. By great good fortune that it was not remodelled and remains a superb example of Jacobean building.

FEATURES

The Council has realised the unique properties of Aston Hall as a historic house and gone to great lengths to furnish it with authentic furniture of the 17th and 18th centuries. They have done a wonderful job. There is a fine collection of portraits, particularly by Gainsborough, Romney, Lely and Kneller. The Romney portrait of Mary Elizabeth Bracebridge, nee Holte, is quite poignant, as her husband's failings led to the house being sold.

Aston Hall is preserved as a "time capsule" of the 17th and 18th centuries. It is the finest Jacobean house in the Midlands and demonstrates the power and wealth of the Stuart gentry.

Attingham Park

WHERE
Map reference SJ 550100; 4 miles south-east of Shrewsbury, on the north side of the old A5, now the B4380.

TRANSPORT
Attingham is close to the M54 via the B5061 and B4380. Buses from Shrewsbury to Telford and Wellington pass close by, and also pass Shrewsbury Railway Station, - enquiries 01743 253030. Park in the grounds.

ACCESS & FACILITIES
National Trust own the house and normally open the grounds and deer park daily from dawn to dusk, except on Christmas Day; enquiries 01743 709203.

A tea room serves light lunches when the house is open, and there are picnic sites. WCs are in the house. Separate tickets are available to the Park and house, NT members enter free.

HISTORY
Attingham was built by the 1st Lord Berwick (Noel Hill) when he inherited the estate from his father in 1783-85. He hired the Scottish architect George Steuart to replace the family home, Tern Hall, and make it look imposing from the Watling Street bridge across the river Tern at Atcham, a mile east. Steuart succeeded brilliantly, with a 400 foot long classical facade which is most impressive from the road. Berwick's successors employed the finest designers of the Regency period to complete the interior and the park, making the estate an very fine example of late neo-classical architecture.

Noel Hill was a member of the Hill family who were important in North Shropshire life from the Tudor times to the 20th century. The Hills were descended from Rowland Hill of Hawkstone, who acquired that estate in 1556. His successors made Hawkstone and its park one of the most amazing creations of the 18th century.

The Attingham branch of the family did not make any attempt to rival Hawkstone until Noel Hill inherited the estate. A figure of national importance, he was made a Baron by Pitt for services rendered as an MP from 1768 to 1784. He had already started work on building Attingham in February 1783 and it was

Attingham Park, Shropshire

finished in 1785. The 2nd Lord Berwick, Thomas Hill, furnished the house with Italian treasures gained on the Grand Tour
and hired Humphrey Repton (whose Red Book is preserved
in the house) to landscape the park in 1797-98. The value of his
artistic acquisitions brought him to employ John Nash to build
a staircase and picture gallery from 1805 to 1807. The result
was financially disastrous, and in 1827 the contents of the
house had to be sold to pay Berwick's debts.

Thomas was succeeded by his brother, William, who spent
twenty five years as a diplomat in Italy acquiring much art.
When he inherited in 1832 he furnished the house with his
possessions, but the estate did not recover from the financial
collapse of 1827. After William's death in 1842 the Berwick's
chose to live in Cronkhill, the house built by Nash for the
agent of the estate. This was the first Italianate villa built
in England - a forerunner of Barry's Trentham. Attingham
was let or shut up for long periods and therefore escaped
the attentions of Victorian fashion. Not until 1919 did the
8th Lord Berwick re-occupy his ancestors' home. His marriage to Theresa Hulton, daughter of a painter, led to a
sensitive revival of the house, which they occupied through
World War II. When Lord Berwick died in 1947 he left the
house and estate to the National Trust.

DESCRIPTION
The exceptional value of Attingham lies less in the architecture of the house, which is indifferent neo-classicism, than in
its Regency interior and Repton's park. Thomas Hill and his
brother's expensive tastes were financially damaging but make
Attingham a Regency treasure house. The gallery for which
Nash was employed lost its original pictures in the sale of
1827, but as restocked by William

it wonderfully represents the taste of an aristocratic collector who had been on the Grand Tour. The dining room was redecorated while Nash worked in the house and is particularly splendid. The drawing room represents the elegant Italian tastes of William who placed there the best of his paintings and furniture. An equally striking reminder of the riches available to a leading servant of the Crown in the early 19th century is the magnificent collection of silver in the Vaults. An ambassador in 1810 would have been supplied with 6,000 oz of silver to create silverware on a scale to impress foreigners. The result is that here we have the work of the finest silversmiths of the age.

The Park as landscaped by Repton has great charm but is less spectacular than Hawkstone and far less consciously landscaped than classical revival parks like Shugborough or Chillington. Even so, it was an important factor in the building of Attingham. Work was in hand from 1769 and in 1772, the turnpike road (Watling Street) and bridge over the Tern were moved south to extend the Park in front of the house. When Humphrey Repton arrived in 1797, he had the River Tern altered to give a smoother circuit of the house, with a weir to maintain the water level and a cascade visible from the house to give interest. These points give a splendid view to the front of the house, but the woods and walks on both flanks and at the rear are equally attractive. Take a stroll around the grounds, which are a pleasant experience in themselves and a sample of the 18th century view of landscape.

Benthall Hall

WHERE
Map reference SJ 658026: 1 mile north-west of Broseley in the Severn Valley, east of Ironbridge.

TRANSPORT
Buses to Telford, Wellington and Bridgnorth run through to Broseley,- enquiries 01743 253030. There are railway stations at Telford, Oakengates and Wellington. There is limited free parking 150 yards from the house.

ACCESS & FACILITIES
A National Trust property open for part of the week in Spring, Summer and Autumn; get details on 01952 882159. NT members enter free. There are WCs, but no cafe or picnic space.

HISTORY

Benthall Hall is a most charming, stone built Elizabethan manor house, with a small but unusually fine Victorian Garden made by the tile manufacturer, George Maw. It has a pleasing Restoration country church in the grounds, and on a fine summer's afternoon is blissfully tranquil. But this idyllic rural scene has a history reaching back to the middle ages, and was linked with some of the pivotal events in the bloody Civil War.

The present house is a classic, late Tudor stone house, rumoured to have been built in 1535 but largely in the style of the 1580s. Records have been lost, but there are indications of substantial rebuilding which is traditionally dated to 1583. This is supported by the large number of priest holes - hiding places for Roman Catholic priests. These would not have been needed in 1535, but were a feature of Catholic Houses after the Reformation outlawed Catholicism. And Benthall was a strongly Catholic house.

A chapel stood here in 1221, and a house linked to one Anfrid de Benetala may have existed as early as 1100. His family were connected with the site, though it was at one time owned by Robert Burnell of Acton Burnell, one of whose descendants (named Philip

Benthall Hall, Shropshire

Burnell de Benethale in a document dated 1322) united the two families. For the next three centuries they lived in obscurity until the Civil War thrust them into the limelight. Lawrence Benthall fortified his house for the King, many of whose supporters were Catholics. But Parliamentary forces occupied the strategically important building and resisted a Royalist attack in 1645.

After the King's execution in 1649 his son, the future Charles II, led a rebellion in 1651. His army was destroyed at the Battle of Worcester and he fled to Boscobel, the remote house north-west of Wolverhampton which had been turned by the Catholic Giffard family of Chillington into a seminary for priests. To reach the sanctuary offered by Lawrence Benthall and his house, Charles headed west to cross the River Severn. However, Parliamentary forces were guarding the river at Madeley and the King returned to Boscobel. Benthall could easily have played the part that Bos-cobel and Moseley Old Hall subsequently did in the adventure, since Lawrence Benthall was related to the Giffards and their coat of arms still ornaments the overmantel in the Entrance Hall.

Benthall then retreated into obscurity, until in 1845 it was sold by descendants of the Benthall's to the local Willey family. From 1845 to 1930 it was occupied by tenants, one of whom was the local tile manufacturer and botanist George Maw who established the present Victorian garden with a collection of rare plants. Meanwhile the Benthall family maintained its interest in this lovely old house, and in 1934 Mrs Mary Clementina Benthall bought it. She was descended from John Pendrel, one of the Boscobel brothers of 1651. In 1958 Mrs Benthall gave the house to the National Trust and she died in 1960, twenty seventh in line from Anfrid de Benethala. Her cousin Sir Paul Benthall became the first tenants of the Trust, and were succeeded in 1985 as tenants by their second son and his wife.

DESCRIPTION
It is easy to see why the Benthall family have maintained links with the Hall. This is not a stately home, but a lived in residence of well to do people with taste. The ground floor is largely furnished from the early 17th century with interesting panelling of that period. Upstairs, the drawing room is fully panelled with a fine Italian plaster ceiling and frieze, and has 17th and 18th century furniture. Next door the library or Great Chamber has many family portraits, giving an unusual feeling of intimacy despite the room's formality. Architecturally the most interesting feature of the house is the oak staircase - apparently built in 1618, and so much a smaller version of that at Aston Hall that it must have been a prototype. The cantilever construction lightens a heavy oak structure.

Outside, the contribution of the many tenants gives the house an added dimension, especially that of George Maw. His successors, Robert Bateman and his wife, laid out pleasing terraces and rockeries. The work of these eminent Victorians was rescued from neglect by Sir Paul and Lady Benthall in the 1960s, and contributes wonderfully to the charm of the place.

Blakesley Hall

WHERE
Map reference SP 130862; 4 miles east of Birmingham City Centre by the A4040 Outer Ring Road.

TRANSPORT
There are lots of buses, including the famous No.11 patrolling the Outer Circle - enquiries 0121 200 2700. The nearest railway station is Stechford, .75 mile away. The Hall is badly signposted but the entrance is in Blakesley Road, and in walking distance of Yardley village and its mediaeval church. There is limited free parking in Blakesley Road.

ACCESS & FACILITIES
The Hall is operated by Birmingham City Council; details of opening hours can be obtained from 0121 783 2193 or 0121 235 1675. At the time of writing entry is free. There are WCs but no refreshments.

HISTORY
Blakesley Hall is pretty well untouched by history and gives its own fascinating glimpse into the lives of the lower gentry, the English middle class, from Tudor times to the 20th century.

Richard Smalbroke was a Birmingham hardware manufacturer and farmer who later imported fine cloths and spices. However, he moved back to rural Yardley to buy land - the only form of real security in Tudor England. By the time of his death, money and large property holdings had won him recognition as a Gentleman. It was his son, also Richard, who continued the business and built Blakesley Hall in 1590. Their family name is preserved in one of the City's main streets. The records of the occupants of the house in the centuries which followed are sparse, but we know of Richard's granddaughter Barbara, who married twice and had twelve children by her second husband. Her eldest son was Aylmer Foliot who inherited in 1679, and left a detailed inventory of the house contents when he died in 1684.

Henry Greswolde, Rector of Solihull, bought the Hall in 1685 and left a fine tomb in Yardley Church. After him for two centuries the Hall was let to farmers or townsmen like Thomas Merry, a paint manufacturer who brought it in 1901. In 1932 the Common Good Trust purchased the house and presented it to Birmingham Corporation, by which time it was an island of antiquity in a suburban sea. Blakesley Hall survived a German air raid in 1941 but lost its roof and suffered damage to the frame. Modern steel columns now stand in the hall and parlour.

Blakesley means literally, the black "ley". or forest clearing, and in spite of modern Yardley's urban sprawl, the splendour of the timber framing shows there was an oak wood nearby. Blakesley Hall remains an excellent example of a timber framed house.

DESCRIPTION
Blakesley is a two storied house with a traditional high pointed roof. It is architecturally typical of its type but exceptionally well preserved. The timber framing is held together with wooden joints and closed with pegs, with width up to 20 feet limited by the length of local timber. The infill panels between the frame were made from split oak and woven hazel, then filled with cow dung and hair before limewashing to keep out the weather. The chimneys were of course built of brick. Around 1650 a brick kitchen wing extension was built, with a bell on the gable end which was used within living memory to call in the labourers.

The ground floor has a Hall, with a long table from 1620- 50, used alternately as the main eating room and a sitting room. The Great Parlour may once have been used as a bedroom, but is now furnished as a sitting room. The best features of the house are the first floor bedrooms. The Painted Chamber is decorated with wall paintings. The bed and its coverings show the room as it would have been in 1684, according to Aymer Foliot's inventory. Beds were highly valued and often left in wills, as in Shakespeare's case. Accurate reproduction bedding has been used to furnish the Second Bedchamber. In the corridor is a brick lavatory shaft.

In the Kitchen wing of 1650 is a cheese press which was listed in the inventory of 1684. Separate rooms were a buttery for dairy products, a still house for distilling, and a boulting house for making flour and bread. These illustrate the main foods of the period, roast beef in Merry England was a luxury, whatever the music hall song says. The servants' chamber is over the kitchen in the new wing. Unlike the great stately homes, servants lived in intimate contact with the families.

Boscobel House

WHERE
WHERE
Map reference SJ 836082; 6 miles north-west of Wolverhampton and
2.5 miles east of Tong. You can reach it from the A5 at Ivesty Bank
or the A41 at Albrighton; it is signposted.

TRANSPORT
There are no buses. Park by the house.

ACCESS & FACILITIES
Boscobell House is run by English Heritage; get details of opening
and admission charges on 01902 850244. There is a pleasant cafe,
WCs and a gift shop.

The house is near Weston Park and Chillington Hall, so it can form
an alternative when their grounds are too wet to walk.

HISTORY
Boscobel House on the Staffordshire/Shropshire border is the site
of one of the most famous incidents in English History - Charles
II's night in the oak tree while escaping from the Battle of Worcester in 1651. Yet while the Royal Oak has become the name of
countless pubs, the actual place is neither impressive not historic.
You can sense this from pictures, which usually look as though
the artist or photographer has featured the kitchen range instead
of the front. Like Moseley Old Hall but more so, Boscobel and
neighbouring White Ladies Priory are quite nondescript.

Originally this was a small, timber framed, two storey house in a
remote wooded area on the eastern border of Shropshire. We do
not know when it was built, but it may have been a hunting lodge
of the Catholic Giffard family of Chillington Hall, and set deep in
the forest. The main body of the house is at right angles to the
timber framed lodge and is traditionally ascribed to John Giffard
of the nearby White Ladies House, which was built close to the
remains of the old priory. White Ladies House has long vanished.

In 1651 Boscobel was owned by Frances, daughter of John Giffard,
and her husband John Cotton. After defeat at Worcester, Charles
Giffard, a member of Charles II's entourage, recommended the King
to flee north to White Ladies. From there Charles decided to escape
by heading west across the River Severn (probably via Benthall Hall)
to Wales. At Madeley he learnt that Parliamentary troops guarded the

river crossings and doubled back, this time to Boscobel. Here he spent the day of September 6th hiding in the branches of the oak. Two days later Charles left to head for Moseley Old Hall north of Wolverhampton, and eventually into exile.

Boscobel then lapsed into obscurity. In 1648 it passed into the hands of Basil Fitzherbert of Norbury and Swynnerton by marriage, perhaps because of the Catholic connection. His family let it to tenants until 1812 when it was bought by Walter Evans, who tried to restore it as it had been in 1651. However the house had become a working farm, and no amount of reconstruction could change that. Evans dressed the house up, painting brickwork to look like half timbering and introducing many anachronistic details. The Earl of Bradford bought the house in 1918 and gave it to the Ministry of Works in 1954. The poor oak had long since suffered terminally from its fame. As early as 1680 the Fitzherberts had to build a wall to protect it from souvenir hunters, and by 1706 writers mention two trees inside the wall, an old decaying tree and a new one growing from the acorn of the old. It is almost certainly this new oak which is preserved today.

DESCRIPTION
Boscobel House is almost entirely a 19th century farm, with stucco covering the 16th and 17th century half timbered elements. This is almost certainly an 18th century device to conceal the fact that parts of the timber framing had decayed and were being replaced with brick. The windows have been changed, the roof altered, and the upper part of the chimney stack rebuilt. While there are some genuinely interesting antique elements, and two concealed rooms or priest holes, you must tax your imagination to capture the house as it was at its moment of fame. Despite a noble attempt to create a box parterre in place of the old formal garden, the house would not be recognised by Charles II. Nevertheless, the romantic associations of Boscobel (from the Italian *bosco bello* - in fair woods) are strong enough to give the place enduring interest.

Chillington Hall

WHERE
Map reference SJ 862069; 4 miles south-west of the A5/A449 junction, (Gailey roundabout). It is not well signposted until one is on top of the entrances from Coven or Boscobel.

TRANSPORT
No buses. Park near the house.

ACCESS & FACILITIES
The house is still owned by the Giffard family and access to both park and house is restricted. For information on opening hours and entry charges phone 01902 850236. There are no refreshments, WCs are at the discretion of the owners, but you can buy a small guide-book. The estate is a family enterprise with a quality all its own.

HISTORY
Chillington Hall is the ancestral home of the Giffard family, who have held the estate since 1178. They originated in Normandy and accompanied William the Conqueror in 1066. The present house is a Georgian building erected between 1724 and 1789. It stands on the site of two previous houses, a mediaeval building and a Tudor house built in the mid-16th century. The house is interesting, but the outstanding feature of the estate is the park, landscaped by Capability Brown and with classical monuments which make it as interesting as the more famous Shugborough.

The Giffards were a notable Staffordshire family in the Middle Ages, and reached a peak of fame and influence under Sir John Giffard, who became a favourite at the court of Henry VIII. He was a notable warrior who carried the Royal Banner when the English army marched out of Calais in 1513.

Sir John features in the legend of Giffard's Cross. He is said to have brought back a panther from his travels, but it escaped. Sir John and his son Thomas hunted the creature, and as it was about to pounce on a woman and child, Sir John shot it dead with an arrow. As his father took aim Thomas is supposed to have shouted *"Prenez haleine, tirez fort"* (Take breath, pull strong). It says much for Sir John's aim and concentration that this silly and ungrammatical interruption did not deliver the panther another meal. The phrase is now the family motto. A wooden cross at the lodge gates marks the spot where the panther was doing its thing, while Sir John is said to have been standing at the front of the house, a mile away.

The Giffard's benefited from the dissolution of the monasteries, buying the old monastic sites of Whiteladies in Shropshire and Blackladies in Staffordshire, where younger branches of the family settled. However the Giffard's were staunch Catholics and refused to follow Henry VIII or Elizabeth I in their break with Rome. A younger son, Gilbert Giffard, became implicated in the plots of Mary Queen of Scots in the 1580s, while the hunting lodge Boscobel became a sanctuary for priests and was involved in the escape of Charles II after the Battle of Worcester.

In 1718 Chillington passed to Peter Giffard of Chillington, and the history of the present Georgian house and estate began. Part of the Tudor house was demolished and replaced in 1724 by the existing south front of three storeys in red brick, probably by Francis Smith of Warwick. The remaining Tudor house was replaced between 1786 and 1789 by Sir John Soane, who was employed by Peter Giffard's grandson, Thomas. Soane incorporated the 1724 south range with two new wings, and the new entrance front with its portico. The portico is similar to Soane's later portico for the Bank of England, and the columns are of huge drums of creamy Tunstall stone. The Ionic capitals are designed after those of the Temple of Fortune in Rome.

Peter Giffard also began creating the long avenue of oak trees which formed the original approach to the house. However, the major work to the park was carried out by Capability Brown during the 1770s for Peter Giffard's son, Thomas Giffard the elder. He employed not only Capability Brown, but also James "Athenian" Paine. Soane is said to have contributed the mock Grecian Temple which stands near Brown's dam. The centrepiece of Brown's landscape is the lake, known as the Pool, which seems wholly natural but was created by building a large dam on which the path runs, to turn three small lakes into one.

Paine described the Pool as "one of the finest pieces of water, within an inclosure, that this kingdom produces; the verges of which are bounded by fine plantations, intermixed with groves of venerable stately oaks". He was correct. The 4 mile walk along the canal and round the Pool on a fine tranquil evening is one of the most pleasant experiences that any Park in this book can offer.

DESCRIPTION
The exterior of the house is not architecturally distinguished; even Soanes' portico looks out of place on a country mansion. But the interior is a fine example of Georgian craftwork and almost on a

par with Attingham. The entrance hall embodies the clean lines
and sense of space of Georgian interior design at its best, while
the dining room on the right of the entrance in Soane's part of the
house is characteristic of the 1780s. This room contains portraits of
the three Giffard's who remodelled Chillington, Peter who started
rebuilding the house, Thomas who employed Capability Brown, and
his son Thomas who employed Soane. The staircase has a block of its
own attached to the south range of the house and is a fine example of
Georgian work, but the crowning joy is the saloon. This was built on
the site of the great hall of the Tudor house and has a roof of many
curves typical of Soane's work, notably the old Bank of England.

However, the treasure of Chillington is Capability Brown's landscape.
Brown's genius was to make highly artificial landscape seems natural,
and here he succeeded brilliantly. The dam at the south of his lake,
and the artificial bridge at the north, both seem to grow out of the
landscape, though they are calculated works of engineering.

The Park contains two other engineering feats. The M54 runs through
the grounds but it is skilful concealed in a deep cutting. One's eye
is taken instead by Brown's sham white house across the motorway,
or Soane's Greek temple on its edge, and is oblivious to the roaring
traffic. There is something similar on the eastern avenue from the
Coven road which once formed part of the carriage drive. It has now
been abandoned as part of the park and you can follow the mile long
public footpath to meet a stately classical bridge over the Shropshire Union Canal. They were built in 1826 by Thomas Telford.

Chillington Park is a triumph of calculation applied to landscape,
and most satisfying to anyone sensitive to the subtleties of Georgian
park design.

Chillington Hall, Staffordshire

Clive House

WHERE
The house is at College Hill in the centre of Shrewsbury, SY1 1LT.

TRANSPORT
Buses and trains.

ACCESS & FACILITIES
Owned by Shrewbury City Council. Get details of opening hours
and entrance fees from the curator on 01743 354811. There are
no facilities at the house, but pubs, cafes, tea shops and WCs
are all nearby.

HISTORY
Clive House is an 18th century terraced town house in the heart of
Shrewsbury, which is traditionally associated with Clive of India,
though he never lived there. It has been developed by Shrewsbury
Museums Service as a museum of 18th and 19th century Shrewsbury
life. The house is particularly interesting for students of Coalport
china.

The building dates back to mediaeval Shrewsbury and was initially a
timber framed building of the type still found here; Rowley's House
being a good example. Unlike that property, the original 15th and
16th century timber of Clive House was absorbed into the structure
of the present 18th century brick building. Evidence of the earlier
work can be found in the roof trusses.

The 15th century hall house was extended about 1600 and bought
in 1752 by a local businessman, John Oliver, who converted
it into three separate dwellings. He added to the Clive House site
a block of rooms in new brick facing the gardens, then squared off
the new facade by demolishing the southern part of the mediaeval
hall. His architect was probably Thomas Pritchard, best known for
his design of the celebrated Iron Bridge in Coalbrookdale.

The area around College Hill was developed as town houses of
the local gentry. Robert Clive, victor of the Battle of Plassey in
1759, was invited to be Mayor of Shrewsbury in 1762. He leased
the premises to qualify as a resident of the Borough, but never
owned them and lived elsewhere. Despite later criticism, he
remained popular in Shrewsbury and served as its MP and its
Mayor. The house seems to have borne his name ever since.

Clive House remained in private hands. During much of the 19th century it was owned by solicitors, but in 1885 the Shrewsbury Girls' High School was founded here. The building was used for teaching up to 1898, then became a private house and surgery until purchased by the Council in 1965. The house is considered typical of many 18th and 19th century houses, and is being developed as a museum of Shrewsbury life in those days.

DESCRIPTION
The house is notable for its antique furniture and local china of the area, notably Coalport. Two large collections of the local Caughley 18th century soft paste china are kept in the Caughley room, while the Edwardian room features sophisticated Coalport china of that period. This demonstration is continued in the dining room decorated in 18th century style. The Dyas Room is designed to recall a homely drawing room of the 1840s, while the Regency Room features a rather austere period decor and Coalport's earliest wares. The kitchen and children's room (where visitors can play with toys) illustrate ways of life in the days before television.

Dudmaston

WHERE
Map reference SK 745888; about 4 miles south-east of Bridgnorth on the A442.

TRANSPORT
Buses from Kidderminster to Bridgnorth pass on the A442; enquiries 01743 253030. The nearest railway station is 4 miles away at Bridgnorth on the steam hauled Severn Valley Railway; enquiries 01299 401001. Park cars by the house.

ACCESS & FACILITIES
Owned by the National Trust; for details of opening hours and charges for the house and gardens phone 01746 780866. National Trust members enter free. Walks round the estate are free and there is a cafe and WCs.

HISTORY
Dudmaston, at Quatt near Bridgnorth is a somewhat similar house to Chillington. Both have histories dating back to the 12th century, both have had Tudor houses on the site, and both seem to have been designed by Francis Smith of Warwick, a competent but

undistinguished architect. Both are also set in very fine parkland influenced by the ideas of the 18th century, but there the similarity ends. Whereas the early history of Chillington is well documented, that of Dudmaston is obscure. The Wolryche family and their successors did not play a major role in history, and the estate fell on hard times until it was taken over by the National Trust in 1981.

The Dudmaston estate has a continuous history of 850 years and has always passed by descent or devise (will), never by sale. Its early history is that of the Wolryche family and little is known of them or their two earlier houses. Thomas Wolryche, was MP for Bridgnorth in the 1620s, and as a strong Royalist commanded Bridgnorth Castle in the Civil War. It was his son, Thomas, who built the existing house between 1695 and 1701. The inheritance was abused by his son, John, the last baronet, who gambled and drank away the family fortune. When he was drowned in 1723 after returning home drunk from the Chelmarsh Races, the family was bankrupt.

The estate remained bankrupt until in 1774 it passed to William Whitmore. He inherited an empty house because the contents had been sold to pay debts, so very little of the present furniture is earlier than 1774. George Whitmore rescued the situation. By the time his son William Wolryche Whitmore inherited in the 1820s, the estate had money for improvements. The roof and attic were transformed by a local builder, John Smallman, to create a solid, unspectacular house.

The garden and park were products of the 18th century development in landscaping and gardening. In 1777 William Whitmore called in William Eames, a landscape gardener who had worked at Erdigg and Chirk Castle, to create an ornamental lake. This was done in the 1820s when several small pools at the bottom of the splendid valley between the house and the Clee Hills were amalgamated into a large one. The valley south-west of the house known as the Dingle contains a stream feeding the Big Pool, and was transformed into a picturesque garden by the resident gardener, Walter Wood. Wood had known the famous Halesowen garden, The Leasowes, and its creator, William Shenstone's book, *Unconnected Thoughts on Gardening (1764),* was in the Dudmaston library. The 19th century saw a return to more formal gardening. In the 20th century Geoffrey Wolryche-Whitmore used the estate as a model of modern forestry.

The Whitmore and Wolryche-Whitmore families furnished the house extensively in the late 18th century. In the 1960s Sir George and Lady Labouchere made many additions from what they had assembled abroad while on diplomatic service. Lady Labouchere also continued

Dudmaston, Shropshire

a tradition of collecting botanical art inherited from her connection
with the Darby family of Coalbrookdale, which were given with the
house to the National Trust.

DESCRIPTION.
The interior of Dudmaston is remarkable because of the 18th furniture and 20th century art and flower paintings. The later are hung
in the Library and the Dining Room. The house is rich in art, and
two rooms have been converted to galleries of 20th century painting
and sculpture. A further room is a gallery of topographical art, and
a fourth a gallery of botanical art. There are also collections celeb-
rating the connections of the house with Charles Babbage who
founded modern computer science, the Darbys and other leading
Quaker families, and Frances Pitt, a leading woman naturalist
who was master of the Wheatland Hounds.

The gardens around Dudmaston are magnificent, although they
have still to recover from the frost of 1981-82. The National Trust
has done much replanting but they will take years to mature. The
Dingle valley poses a particular problem. For many years it ran
wild, but National Trust volunteers have done excellent work and a
walk through it shows phases of the development of the Dudmaston
landscape. The estate offers two walks of 4 and 5.5 miles through
Geoffrey Wolryche Whitmore's plantations which visit the River
Severn. The woodland is still worked by the National Trust as an
element of the Dudmaston inheritance.

Ford Green Hall

WHERE
Map reference SJ 889509; Ford Green Road, Smallthorne, Stoke on Trent ST6 1NG. This is east of Burslem and just north of the A53.

TRANSPORT
Buses run; enquiries 01785 223344.

ACCESS & FACILITIES
Owned by Stoke on Trent City Council and normally open on afternoons all year round, except for Christmas week; check on 01782 534771. There are limited refreshment facilities and WCs. At the time of writing, admission is free. There is wheelchair access on the ground floor. Free tours on request.

HISTORY
Ford Green Hall was built in 1624 by Hugh Ford and his wife Margery on the site of an earlier farmhouse. The family had been living at Ford Green, a farm east of the town of Burslem, since 1508. The modest 36 acres provided a comfortable living for what would have been a lower middle class family.

The house was enlarged in the 18th century but the core remains largely as built. William and Mary Ford built on the west side in 1728; their son Hugh added an extension to the east in 1734. The direct line of the Ford family ended in 1782 when another William died without male heir, and his youngest daughter sold house and contents in 1803.

The Industrial Revolution flowed around Ford Green Hall as Stoke on Trent expanded and merged with Burslem. The house lost its land and ceased to be a farm, but survived without major alteration through a series of owners. In 1946 the City of Stoke on Trent bought the building and renovated it to regain its appearance as it would have looked to the Ford family. The Hall survived flooding in 1987, and though some of the wattle and daub panels were damaged, it has been well restored as a splended example of a yeoman farmer's house of its period.

DESCRIPTION
The heart of Ford Green Hall is a half timbered yeoman's house of 1624. The 18th century extensions are brick. The timber

framed portion is a typical West Midlands farmhouse of the Jacobean period, with three rooms downstairs and three up. The family made extensive inventories of the contents in wills of 1713 and 1723, and the renovators have tried to furnish it according to those lists.

Like the house itself, most of the furniture is made of oak. The finest piece is a tester (four poster) bed of 1600 - 1650. The hall is furnished to represent the earliest period of the Ford family, with a table of 1650 and a parlour cupboard c1640. It is worth looking for the chest of drawers by the bed in the hall chamber, which is deceptive, because it is a close stool or comode. Sanitation at Ford Green Hall was primitive

Hawkstone Hall and Park

Hawkstone Park with its fantastical collection of scenic oddities was built up gradually from the mid 17th century as a setting for the Hall. Although they are close together, ownership was separated early in the 20th century, and both are so rich in absorbing features that you should not attempt to "do" both in the same trip.

WHERE
Map reference SJ 575295; for both the Hall and the Park head for Marchamley, about 1 mile north-west of Hodnet on the A442.

The entrance to Hawkstone Hall, a mile from the house itself, is at Marchamley village.

The entrance to Hawkstone Park is off the minor road running west from Marchamley to the A49.

TRANSPORT
Buses run; enquiries 01743 253030. Park cars in the grounds of the Hall or Park.

ACCESS & FACILITIES
Hawkstone Hall is now a religious retreat of the Roman Catholic order of Redemptorists, and closed to the public for most of the year. However, it does open for 28 days in the summer, usually in August. For details phone 01630 685242. When open the house provides light refreshments and has WCs.

Hawkstone Park is privately owned and normally open daily from 1st April to 31st October. For details of opening times and admission prices phone 01939 200300/200611. There is a gift shop where you can also buy picnic packs; very useful, because the full tour involves a good walk and can take four hours. Special events are staged. Make sure you use the WCs at the entrance and bring stout footwear.

HAWKSTONE HALL - HISTORY

Hawkstone Hall and Gardens have not shared the national fame of the nearby Park, and have been called "the secret jewel of Shropshire". It is a fair description. The house of the Hill family has existed in quiet obscurity since being divorced from its Park early in the 20th century, a seclusion now preserved by its new owners. When they do open the Hall to the public, a Grade I Georgian mansion is revealed of exceptional calm and beauty.

The ancient Shropshire family of the Hills is connected with both Hawkstone and Attingham Park. The family fortune was made by Sir Rowland Hill, merchant and banker, who became one of the closest supporters of Henry VIII and was the first protestant to become Lord Mayor of London. He invested heavily in land from the dissolution of the monasteries, buying Hawkstone manor for £700 and building a big estate around it. It is this Sir Rowland Hill who is celebrated on the monument in Hawkstone Park.

The family lapsed into obscurity until the end of the 17th century, when the Reverend Richard Hill (1654-1727) inherited the estate. He abandoned a career in the church for politics and diplomacy and was appointed Deputy Paymaster to the forces of William III, his chief patron. Here he used his position to divert public funds into making a huge personal fortune. After retiring in 1708 he devoted his wealth to building up Hawkstone, rebuilding a William and Mary house between 1719 and 1727 to form the central block of the present structure. He was unmarried, but knowing his nephew Rowland would inherit, secured from the Crown a Baronetcy for him to give his heir both a fine house and a title.

Rowland Hill, the 1st baronet, (1705-1783) continued development of the Hall. He built the attic storey and carried up the end bays as small towers with pyramidal roofs, then had the two pavilions built which were linked to the main house by quadrants. Sir Rowland also enlarged the Park to include the mediaeval Red Castle and lay the foundations of the Gothic park. When Dr Johnson visited in 1774 it was already a wonder.

Hawkstone Hall, Shropshire

It was the 2nd Baronet, Sir Richard Hill, (1732-1808), who made
the Park truly notable. He employed the landscape gardener, William
Emes, to build two waterways, Hawk Lake and Menagerie Pool.
At his death in 1808 the Park was attracting a substantial number of
visitors, so a hotel was built for them. The 3rd Baronet left things
much as the first two had made them, but the 4th Baronet, another
Sir Rowland (1800-1875), made alterations, of which the biggest was
an elegant ballroom more in keeping with the 18th century than the
Victorian period. Sir Rowland was the 2nd Viscount, and in trying
to live up to his station ruined the family fortune.

The 3rd Viscount, Rowland Clegg Hill, (1833-95) inherited an estate
in financial trouble. By the time of his death debts were so severe
that everything in the house had to be sold, thus no furniture from
the Hill period survives. The house lay empty until 1906 when the
4th Viscount sold it to the 1st Baron Marchamley of Hawkstone. He
remodelled the pavilions but owned the Hall for only seven years. In
1924 Hawkstone Park Hotel bought the land now occupied by the golf
course. The Hall and surrounding land were bought in 1926 by the
Redemptorist Catholic order, who used it as a seminary.

A Romanesque brick church was built near the house in 1932, and
a students wing in 1962. In 1973 the students moved out and the Hall
became a pastoral centre. English Heritage made grants for essential
structural repairs and renovation of the principal rooms of the house.
In return the house and gardens are now open to the public for 28
days each year.

DESCRIPTION

The outstanding feature of the exterior is the colour scheme, a most unusual blend of red brick with cream painted plaster in which the columns and string courses are picked out. It looks like a richly iced cake, and on a sunny day the house seems to glow. The main west front is particularly stately. A square central block dominated by a pedimented baroque centre-piece is wholly decorated in cream plaster. It rises above the curved quadrants linking the pavilions which jut out before the house to make an almost theatrical enclosure. One expects actors to appear from the doors front and side to act a period piece on the forecourt.

Only the central and southern sections of the ground floor are open to the public. The entrance hall is a pleasing introduction to a splendid and well maintained interior. The saloon behind is Rowland Hill's finest contribution to the house, with a remarkable carved marble fireplace featuring a portrait of Richard Hill, who also appears in a large painting of *The Siege of Namur* alongside William III. The decor of the saloon is probably by Henry Flit-croft, a disciple of the architect William Kent. The decor is heavy classical, especially the medallions of Roman Emperors.

The saloon contrasts with the Wyatt ballroom of the 1830s, done in the style of Louis XIV with stucco by Francis Bernasconi who was the finest stucco artist of the time. The expense of Wyatt's work ruined the estate, but there is no denying the opulence of the ballroom. Less opulent and in many ways more impressive is the conservatory or winter garden built in the southern quadrants. The simple grandeur of this well lit room is enhanced by the plain but effective circular balustrade at the end. This staircase leads up to the billiard room, a spacious and elegant place in which to concentrate on the game.

The rooms open to the public are well preserved reminders of the opulence of the past. But perhaps the garden behind is even more splendid. The formal avenues and terraces have been lovingly and immaculately restored by David and Monica Weller. From 1988 they have worked to restore a garden with a balance of woodland of magnificent trees, rose gardens, plain lawns and herbaceous borders. This tranquillity and beauty is a rich compliment to their work.

HAWKSTONE PARK AND FOLLIES - HISTORY

The 100 rugged acres of Hawkstone Park has attracted much media attention in recent years as one of the most remarkable products of the Romantic landscape garden movement. It has been called a masterpiece of the school of Naturalistic Landscape, which is both apt and misleading. The Park did indeed grow out of the naturalistic movement, but it has little to do with Capability Brown or his school. It is almost unique; a dreamlike Gothic landscape of weird proportions which is listed Grade I landscape in the English Heritage Register. You might see it best as a woodland fantasy of cave, cliffs and grottoes. It does not offer a restful stroll through carefully controlled scenery, but tries to create a wild and rugged environment with elements of fantasy. It was a suitable film location for a TV production of C S Lewis's mystical *Chronicles of Narnia*.

Very little is known about the development of the Park. It is clear the 1st Baronet laid its foundations by buying land to bring the ruined mediaeval Red Castle into the estate. By 1752 it also included Terrace Hill (the main cliff) and Grotto Hill. By 1774, when Dr Johnson visited, the scenery was impressive enough for him to remark on "its prospects, the awfulness of its shades, the horrors of its precipices, the verdure of its hollows and the loftiness of its rocks".

Sir Richard Hill inherited in 1783 at the age of 51. He immediately opened the park to the public and published a guide book. This was successfully sold locally, and in 1784 a second edition sold in London, beginning the Park's national fame. This book listed The Grotto, the Awful Precipice, the Ravens Shelf, a rustic sofa, The Ships Beak, The Retreat, The Grand Valley and the Red Castle with the Giant's Well and Lion's Den. Doctor Johnson had noted that the Park excelled Dovedale but nevertheless "wants water", and this was supplied in 1784 with the construction of the Hawk River.

The Park became a national institution, and by 1799 the local inn had been turned into a hotel for visitors. At the time of Sir Richards' death in 1808 Hawkstone was as much an attraction as Alton Towers today, with an itinerary which included sailing on the Hawk River or walking to the Bury Walls, an Iron Age hill fort, by way of the Citadel, a house built to represent a castle. In the 1840s and early 1850s two new drives were created. One rose to the Terrace while another forged a deep gorge focussing on a dramatic remnant bridge of rock called the Arch, all entirely in keeping with the eighteenth century landscape.

This marked the high point of the development of the Park. The 2nd Viscount Hill who had built the new Drives bankrupted the estate, and the Park was neglected from the mid-19th century. The 3rd Viscount was declared bankrupt in 1894. While new 20th century owners looked after the house and gardens, the Park was ignored and reverted to nature. Nevertheless, the four hills and their unique walks were not damaged, and in 1990 the owners of Hawkstone Park Hotel were able to buy the Park and recreate what it had been at its peak.

DESCRIPTION
Hawkstone Park cannot easily be described. The walk over the four hills crosses steep ravines spanned by wooden bridges suggesting the Swiss Alps, the 30 feet high White Tower, a thatched Temple of Patience (irreverently known as Gingerbread Hall from the days when gingerbread was sold there), an enormous classic Urn, a 200 feet deep Grotto, a 100 feet high monument of 1795 supporting a statue of Sir Rowland Hill (with an interior spiral staircase), a Hermitage (which at one time housed a hairy retainer acting his head off), and the Red Castle. The latter is not currently open to the public. The whole is greater than the sum of the parts, for the dramatic setting of the wooded hills makes a circuit of the Park a magical mystery tour.

Himley Hall

WHERE
Map reference SO 888916; 4 miles west of Dudley near the A449 Wolverhampton to Kidderminster Road. The gate is on the B4176.

TRANSPORT
Buses pass; enquiries 0121 200 2700.

ACCESS & FACILITIES
The Hall was only partly open as we went to press, but for details of its function as a museum, opening hours and facilities, phone 01902 326665. More detailed tours of the building can be arranged. There is no charge for people, but a small parking fee for cars.

HISTORY
Himley Hall is a pale shadow of what was part of one of the richest estates in the country. Belonging to the Ward family of Dudley who had three major houses, it has been overshadowed by their mediaeval home at Dudley Castle and the magnificent Witley Court where they lived in the 19th century. Yet it did have a period of magnificence between the wars, and while the family and the elegance are long gone, you can still hear echoes. Hopefully as Dudley Borough

Himley Hall, Staffordshire

Council convert the estate to museum and leisure use, they can capture some of this history for future generations.

The history of the Dudleys and Dudley Castle goes back to the Norman Conquest, but that of Himley Hall starts in 1628. In that year Edward Sutton, last Earl of Dudley, gave his only surviving legitimate heir Frances Sutton in marriage to Humble Ward, who was son of the court jeweller William Ward. This dynastic marriage enabled the estate to meet the Earl's enormous debts. The Ward family owned Himley Manor, but it was not until Dudley Castle was deliberately ruined by Parliamentary forces in the Civil War that Frances and her husband moved to Himley, and it became the family's main seat. Charles I slept there in 1645 on the way to the Battle of Naseby.

The old manor house was swept away in 1740 when it was inherited by John Ward, a cousin not in direct line of descent. He became the first Viscount Dudley and Ward in 1763, but despite his importance little is known of the house. It was his eldest son John inheriting in 1774 who began the changes which made the Himley Hall we see today. Britain was undergoing the Industrial Revolution, and John Ward joined in by enclosing most of the open fields on his estates. This was more than an agricultural advantage, for the area was rich in coal and iron ore and well on the way to becoming the Black Country.

John Ward ensured that the land around his seat remained unspoiled, and immediately employed Capability Brown to remodel the estate. As at Chillington, Brown's main contribution was to create a large lake. Unlike Chillington, the lake was integrated into a landscape including the house, with a splendid vista from the terrace of the west front which sweeps across a haha to the lake half a mile away. Houses to the south were cleared as parkland was created, and the road to Dudley was realigned further from the house. Himley thus became a classic late 18th century landscape with the house standing in isolation, albeit without the popular resistance encountered by many enclosures. It remains much as Brown intended.

John Ward was succeeded in 1823 by his nephew John William, 4th Viscount. John William extensively rebuilt the house in 1824-27 to create the present building. The old model of a central block with low wings, like Shugborough, was abandoned and the house was extended as a C plan structure with neo-classical facade. The 4th Viscount became Foreign Secretary in 1827 but showed such signs of mental strain that he lasted only a year. His second cousin the Rev William Humble Ward inherited Himley in 1833 but showed marked signs of madness, so the estate was put in trust for his children. None of this affected the value of the estate, which grew as the Industrial Revolution created the Black Country.

However, industrialisation took its toll. In 1836 Sir Steven Glynne began to develop the Oak Farm Estate south-west of Himley as an ironworks. The previous year William Ward, 16 year old son of the eccentric Reverend had inherited the estate, but he found the noise and smoke from the ironworks intolerable. Lord Ward escaped from Himley by purchasing the Witley Estate in Worcestershire for the astonishing price of £667,000. Industry had made the Wards one of the richest families in the country, though they had no intention of living anywhere near the source of their wealth. Lord Ward moved to Witley and Himley became a second home.

In 1865 Lord Ward's wealth and status earned him an Earldom, and by this time he was one of the richest men in the country, with over 25,000 acres in Britain and other interests abroad. However, the family history mirrored that of the country as a whole as imperial priorities and economic decline sapped the national vigour. The 2nd Earl turned to politics and became Lord Lieutenant of Ireland in 1902, and Governor General of Australia in 1908. This was unfortunate for the estate, for it was facing both British agricultural decline and commercial competition from the more advanced industries of Germany and USA. The need for economy after World War I forced the Wards to sell Dudley House in London and Witley Court, and one of the five largest fortunes in the country was materially reduced.

But all things are relative. When the Wards returned to Himley it became a splendid seat as they poured what was still a fortune into modernising the house. The 2nd Earl (died 1932) and his son were close to the Royal Family and the Royal brothers often stayed at the house. The Prince of Wales (later Edward VIII) landed his private plane on the front lawn. In 1934 the Duke of Kent and Princess Marina of Greece spent two weeks of their honeymoon at Himley. Today it is hard to see the attraction; Dudley and district are interesting but not pretty, and the surrounding landscape is unspectacular. But Himley was clearly a luxurious retreat with tennis, shooting, fishing, riding and boating.

The luxury did not last. During World War II the family moved out and the house was used as a Red Cross hospital. When peace returned the family did not, and in 1947 the Hall and grounds were sold to the Coal Board. After use as offices, the Board sold the estate to Dudley and Wolverhampton Councils in 1967, and on 5th August 1967 the Park was opened to the public.

DESCRIPTION
Himley Hall is partly closed to the public as we prepare for the press (August 1996), and is being converted into a glass museum by Dudley Council. (Stourbridge and Brierley Hill are world famous for cut glass.) They promise to restore eight rooms of the historic core to their former glory, to provide a new quality venue to exhibitions conferences and prestige events. It is hoped that this will offer an opportunity to recall the history of the Ward family, and perhaps even the moral implicit in the rise of the family fortune and its subsequent decline. The Council is also intent on managing the parkland round the Hall to re-establish as far as possible the Capability Brown landscape.

Izaac Walton's Cottage

WHERE
Map reference SJ 875290; 4 miles north-west of Stafford and just north of the A5013 at Little Bridgeford. This is 3 miles north-west of Junction 14 on the M6. The cottage stands near where the road crosses the railway.

TRANSPORT
Norton Bridge railway station is about .5 mile north. Buses from Stafford to Eccleshall pass on the A5013; enquiries 01785 223344.

ACCESS & FACILITIES
Get details of opening times and entrance fees on 01785 240204. There are toilets at the cottage but normally no refreshments.

HISTORY

Izaac Walton is best known as author of *The Complete Angler*. He was born in Stafford in 1593, but his birthplace in the town centre was knocked down in 1888 and replaced by the Police Station. He spent his early adult years in London, retiring to Stafford in 1644 with a modest fortune. His retirement may have been partly due to his support for the Royalist cause in the Civil War. He lived at Shallowford intermittently at this time.

Little is known of the cottage before Walton lived in it during the Civil War. It is an attractive timber framed building with a thatched roof and similar to thousands of modest houses of the type owned by the lower gentry in the 16th and 17th centuries. The Oak House in West Bromwich and Blakesley Hall are grander examples of the same type. Izaac Walton's cottage is much smaller, being more on the scale of the original Ford Green Hall in Stoke. To us the house seems cramped, but unlike the one or two roomed labourers' cottages of the time, Walton had a modest degree of space and comfort. A major attraction to Walton was the nearby Meece Brook, a favourite angling haunt which is mentioned in his poem "The Angler's Wish" in *The Compleat Angler*.

When he died in 1683 Walton left the property at Shallowford to the Town and Corporation of Stafford for charitable purposes. The Stafford Charity Trustees administered the property until 1920 when responsibility was transfered to the County Council. Fire damage caused by a spark from a passing steam train in 1927 required repair. In 1939 the thatched roof was replaced by tiles but the thatch was subsequently restored.

DESCRIPTION

This small house has a boxed timber frame with wide plastered infil panels. The thatched roof spreads like a floppy pancake over the eaves, beneath which tiny upper storey windows peer cautiously. It squats in a little hedged plot as if it has grown there. All the rooms are tiny, but an interesting feature is an even smaller one set off the entrance hall which contains a fireplace. No more than half a dozen people could have squeezed in.

The cottage was never Walton's permanent home and contains no contemporary object associated with him. The aim of the museum is to show a typical late 17th century domestic interior such as Walton would have known. The cottage also houses an angling museum demonstrating the development of the craft since Walton's time. There is a 17th century herb garden, a picnic orchard, and an extensive programme of events.

Moat House

Map reference SJ 494303; Longnor is 8 miles south of Shrewsbury off
the A49 Shrewsbury - Church Stretton road. The Moat House is up a
lane signed "No Through Road". Note that it is only 3 miles west of
Acton Burnell Castle, so you could visit both.

TRANSPORT
Buses pass; enquiries 01743 253030.

ACCESS & FACILITIES
The Moat House is privately owned by Peter and Margaret Richards
who run a Guest House. It is normally open to the public for viewing
on Thursday afternoons, but this should be checked on 01743 718434.
Guest House facilities are open from Spring to Autumn, and given 48
hours notice the Richards's will serve a four course dinner.

HISTORY
Unlike most of the houses in this book, the Moat House in Longnor
near Shrewsbury is not only lived in, but you can briefly inhabit it
for meals and bed and breakfast. Despite being an authentic mediaeval timber framed manor house with a water filled moat and dining
hall with an open fire, this is a guest house with modern convenien-
ces. It is the only Shropshire example of an occupied, timber
framed house of the middle ages within a water filled moat.

The history of the site starts before 1290 when a moat was recorded.
The prospect of Welsh raids across the border made defence a high
priority, and the date is known because the then occupant obtained
Royal permission to double the width to twelve feet. The house
itself was built in 1467, placing it in a period when the site was
owned by Thomas Acton, a member of the well known Shropshire
family which owned land at Acton Pigott and Acton Burnell. His
house was substantial for the time, showing that he had status and
wealth. Acton was a lawyer who was a servant of Lord Talbot,
Earl of Shrewsbury and a Lancastrian. However, he held onto
his land when the Yorkist Edward IV became king.

Moat House became a farm from about 1600 to 1865, and was then
subdivided into two cottages to house farm workers. In 1964 it was
condemned as unfit for human habitation and sold out of the Corbett
Estate. A Mr Rouse bought and restored it to a single dwelling. He
added central heating, uncovered the massive stone fire places built

about 1590, and exposed some of the fine timber work. In 1970 the present owners bought the house and in 1988 started a programme of repair and restoration. With the agreement of English Heritage, they added a small extension at the southern end.

DESCRIPTION
The present building is a two storey box framed structure of the late 15th century, with later stone gables and a 20th century extension. A floor was inserted in the Hall, probably in the late 16th century, to create the upper storey. At the same time a massive stone chimney with four fireplaces was built at the north end of the dining hall. At first floor level the timbers are close studded, but on the ground floor they have been replaced by brick supports. The roof timbers visible in the dining hall once formed the roof of the great hall. Two wooden carved heads on them may be those of the builders.

The rectangular water filled moat encloses some four acres. On the western side is a platform with four poststones standing in it, similar to the gatehouse at Stokesay. The site has been left as a wildlife sanctuary, with many kinds of birds, fungi and plants. The most notable feature is a black poplar 70 feet tall, one of the rarest of native British trees. The house also has a fishpool.

Moreton Corbet Castle, Shropshire

Moreton Corbet Castle

WHERE
Map reference SJ 561232; 8 miles miles north-east of Shrewsbury on
the A53 Shrewsbury to Newcastle road, and 1 mile north of Shawbury.

TRANSPORT
Buses pass; enquiries 01743 253030.

ACCESS & FACILITIES
The site is run by English Heritage and normally open at any reasonable time. For information phone 01604 730320. Entry is free
but there are no refreshments or toilets.

HISTORY
Moreton Corbet Castle, like Acton Burnell Castle, is both a ruin
and a house which is not a castle. Unlike Acton Burnell, it was
once a genuine castle and is built on the ruins of the older building. The original castle was a small marcher stronghold built
probably in the 12th century. It was rebuilt partly in the 1560s,
during the ownership of Sir Andrew Corbet, Vice President of the
Marches who inherited in 1538. Little of this structure survives.

The history is obscure. Sir Andrew Corbet started to build in
1579, but little of his work remains. The impressive south range
was almost certainly inspired by his son, Robert Corbet, who
according to one commentator "carried away with the affectionate
delight of architecture, began to build in a barraine place a most
gorgeous and stately house, after the Italian model; but death
prevented him so that he left the new work unfinished and the
old Castle defaced". This makes sense; Robert Corbet was a
diplomat who travelled in Italy, France and the Low Countries.
He died in 1583 so the idea that he did not finish the building is
consistent. Some of the detail is disorganised and the tall ogee
gables are more appropriate to a date in the early 17th century,
perhaps even 1627, the date of a drawing of the south front made
by John Smythson.

The house was damaged in a Civil War skirmish, the Corbets being
active Royalists, and Parliamentary forces set fire to the building
in September 1644. A drawing records chimney stacks on the south
range bearing the date 1667, suggesting that it was repaired. But by
the 18th century the Corbets had moved out of the building and by
1776 the south range was roofless. When the building was drawn in

the early 19th century it was in much the same condition as today. In 1949 the family gave the ruin to the Ministry of Works (now English Heritage), but ownership remained with the Corbets.

DESCRIPTION
The south range housed a suite of very large chambers, the principal ones on the first floor, of which almost nothing survives. The outer walls however are stately and beautiful. They impressed Pevsner who says, "Architecturally it was amongst the most impressive and consistent designs in the country. It ought to rank with Kirby". He notes that the use of columns in the facade is French, which is unusual in this country but was used at Longleat.

For the non-architect, the pleasure of the house lies in its stateliness and blend of a sophisticated Elizabethan style with the crude remains of the castle. With its ogee gables soaring splendidly, the tall but firmly placed building seems to command its surrounding area like a galleon on a calm sea. On a bright summers day, the whole site gives a calm and pleasing impression. A picnic here is a particularly enjoyable way of spending a relaxing afternoon.

Morville Hall

WHERE
Map reference SK 669940; about 3 miles west of Bridgnorth, by the main A458 road to Much Wenlock and Shrewsbury.

TRANSPORT
Buses to Bridgnorth and Shrewsbury pass; enquiries 01743 253030. There are railway stations in both towns - Bridgnorth (Severn Valley Railway) - 01299 40101, and Shrewsbury - 0121 643 2700.

ACCESS & FACILITIES
The National Trust lease Morville Hall and access for guided tours and refreshments is only by written appointment with the tenant, Mrs J K Norbury, at Morville Hall, Bridgnorth WV16 5BN.

HISTORY
Morville Hall is a most attractive Georgian gentry house in mellow grey stone, which is flanked by two pavilion walls ending in two charming, cupola topped pavilions. The house faces south-east to a most pleasing small church across a ha-ha. Wooded hills flank the house to the west and cows graze the fields in front. The whole

outlook justifies Pevsner's comment; "a beautiful picture from the road". Access is limited and by appointment, but when the house is closed it is still worth stopping.

The original Tudor house was built at the Reformation with stone from a dissolved priory. The current house is a modernised version of the Tudor building, completely Georgianised and not, as the National Trust handbook says, an "Elizabethan house". The alterations were carried out in the 18th century by the Weaver family. Arthur Weaver III inherited the Hall in 1747 and commissioned the architect William Baker of Audlem. Baker was thought to have added the two pavilions and curtain walls, but recent surveys show that he added only the north pavilion; the south pavilion is a Tudor building. The two little buildings are not quite parallel but cleverly splayed out to create a sense of space. Baker changed all the windows to sashes, inserted oak panelling and, it is said, added giant Tuscan doric half columns and pilasters to the fronts of the two wings, to disguise 16th century butresses. However, they are missing from West and Calverts' 1831 picture of the Hall.

A second phase of alteration took place in 1770-1780, when the top floor and graceful classical porch were added. With a three sided bay window in the Drawing Room, they created the 18th century house we see today. It passed out of the Weaver family and was sold to Sir Frederick Acton (father of Lord Acton, the historian), who let it to a succession of tenants. It was then sold to a Midland cinema owner in 1930, who in 1936 sold it to Dr W J S Bythell. The Hall was given to the National Trust by his daughter Audrey in 1966 with 140 acres. Members of the family still live there.

DESCRIPTION
The most notable feature of the house is the plasterwork of the kitchen ceiling, which was part of the Tudor house and done in the 1580s. It is so similar to plaster ceilings at Wilderhope Manor, eight miles away, and nearby Upton Cresset Hall, that the same hands may have been at work. George Smyth who owned the Hall in this period was the son of Frances Cresset of Upton Cresset. In the re-entrant angles of the front east facade are the Elizabethan staircase turrets, where the original windows can be seen blocked up.

A mid-18th century picture by John Inigo Richards of the grounds to the east of the house shows the semicircular lawn and drive very much as they are to-day. This splendid vista is immaculately maintained by the National Trust. The garden to the south is being restored from the 1790s plan, which shows a a closed rectangle formed by the house, two rows of yews and a mediaeval stewpond which was canalised in the 18th century. A former rose garden is being laid out as a parterre to a design based on the plasterwork of the kitchen ceiling, while new formal gardens are being laid out on the north side of the Hall. The grounds are delightful.

Moseley Old Hall

WHERE
Map reference SJ 932043; in Moseley Old Hall Lane, Fordhouses, Wolverhampton, about 4 miles north of the town centre and just north of the M54. Get there from Junction 1 (A460) or 2 (A449). It is signed from the A449 Wolverhampton to Stafford road.

TRANSPORT
Buses pass on the A460 and A449: enquiries 01785 223344.

ACCESS & FACILITIES
A National Trust property and open on their usual lines; enquiries 01902 782808. There is a tea room in an 18th century barn, WCs and a shop. The Hall has an extensive programme of educational, cultural and living history events.

HISTORY
Moseley Old Hall is one of the National Trust's less interesting properties but formally listed as, ".... an Elizabethan House with later alterations. Charles II slept here after the Battle of Worcester and the bed is on view, as well as his hiding place. The small garden has been recreated in 17th century style with formal box parterre". While all this is true, it suggests more of a period piece than actually exists. Like other houses linked to Charles II after the Battle of Worcester, Northycote Farm and Boscobel House, very little of the Civil War period survives at Moseley. It requires an effort of the imagination to recreate the events of the 1650s.

The original timber framed house was built around 1600 for Henry Pitt of Bushbury, Wolverhampton, a merchant. It was inherited through marriage by the Whitgreave family who held the house till 1925 when it was sold. From about 1820, however, the house was deserted by the family who moved half a mile to the nearby new Moseley Court. About 1870 the outer walls of the Old Hall were replaced by brick, giving it the appearance

of a Victorian farm house which it has today. In 1962 the
virtually empty hall was given to the National Trust.
Almost all the furniture and pictures now shown have been
lent or given to them.

Although externally the house is Victorian, internally it is the
least altered of the surviving "Charles II" houses. The King
stayed at Moseley for two nights, September 8th and 9th 1651,
after his unsuccessful attempt to cross the River Severn. He
had earlier stayed at Boscobel but been forced to head east.
Thomas Whitgreave was a loyal Royalist who was willing to
harbour the King, but he had to hide in a priesthole on the
afternoon of the 9th when unsuspecting

Moseley Old Hall, Wolverhampton

(66)

Parliamentary soldiers passed by. The presence of the priesthole underlines the fact that the Whitgreaves were Catholics. Charles later escaped via Bristol, but he never forgot the circumstances of his escape. When he lay dying it was John Huddlestone, the Chaplain at Moseley, who he called for to give him the last rites.

There are reports that Moseley Old Hall is haunted. Witnesses have spoken of animals behaving as if they were frightened by something invisible, and of objects disappearing and reappearing. Most interesting was the shadowy figure of a man who sat on a bed reading, which has been seen several times. It would be nice to announce that this was Charles II studying maps, but the figure bears no resemblance to the King and there is really no evidence to connect them. A detailed account appears in *Midland Ghosts & Hauntings* by Anne Bradford & Barry Roberts (QuercuS).

DESCRIPTION
The tour of the house starts at the heavy, studded back door through which Charles entered on September 8th 1651. It follows the King's route up the backstairs to the so called King's room. Dominating it is the four poster bed he used, which was sold to the Manders of Wightwick in 1935 and presented back by Lady Mander in 1962. The panelling of the room was sold in the 1920s and has not been replaced. In the floor of the cupboard next to the fireplace is the priesthole in which Charles hid.

The rest of the house is much altered from Charles' days. A corridor has been inserted next to the main bedroom, and the chapel in which John Huddlestone celebrated services was then open to the rafters. The fine portraits dotting the walls have nearly all been brought to the house in recent years. A particularly interesting feature is the half timbering which can be seen on the main stair, the Elizabethan star chimneys, and the interior wall wattle and daub, now very fragile. There is much to see of the Stuart period at Moseley Old Hall, but relatively little of the contents is of that time.

The National Trust have made the best use they could of the limited garden available. The arbour is copied from one in Thomas Hill's *A Gardener's Labyrinth,* and the plants were all grown in the Stuart period. The finest feature of the garden is the carefully created Knot Garden, a pattern made with dwarf box and filled in with coloured gravel. Box spheres on stems give an added dimension to the exercise. On the wall of the house is grown the Musk Rose Rosa Moschata, known in England since the days of Elizabeth I.

Northycote Farm

Map reference SO 934025; in the Bushbury suburb of Wolverhampton,
3 miles north of the centre and midway between the A460 and A449.

TRANSPORT
Buses run nearby; enquiries 0121 200 2700. The nearest railway
station is Wolverhampton.

ACCESS & FACILITIES
Northycote farm is owned by Wolverhampton Borough Council. For
details of opening hours, admission charges and events phone 01902
397906. There are WCs and a tearoom.

HISTORY
Northycote Farm is the least known of the group of houses associated
with Charles II's escape after the Battle of Worcester in 1651. Now
in the outskirts of Wolverhampton, the Farm is the centre of an 80
acre Country Park devoted to livestock. Its core is the two storey
timber framed building of c1600 which Charles II visited before
going on to Moseley Old Hall a mile away.

The timber framed building stands at the extreme south-west corner
of the recently destroyed Moseley Court in Wolverhampton's suburb
of Bushbury. It was probably built around 1600 as an entrance lodge
for Moseley Old Hall, but the early history is obscure. It was associated with a family called Underhill, who though Roman Catholics,
refused entrance to Charles II in his famous flight. The King then
headed north to Moseley Old Hall, where he was sheltered by
Thomas Whitgreave.

There is very little of the 17th century left at Northycote but it is
a substantial yeoman's house of some interest. By 1666 Thomas
Underhill paid hearth tax on five hearths, but though the main
chimney block has five stacks these serve only two hearths. It
is assumed the others were in another building. The house consists
of six bays. Bay number 1 at the west end is a separate building
not open to the public and rebuilt in the 19th century, but the
timber frame is part of the main structure. Bay 6 was rebuilt in
1758 and a stone tablet set high in the wall has the initials of
John and Winifred Underhill who carried out the work.

The Whitgreaves bought the building and seem to have converted it into a farm around 1820. They built a new house - Moseley Court - with a new entrance lodge, and moved from Moseley Old Hall in that year. The old building was surrounded by new farm buildings in the 19th century and was let to tenants until 1922, when the Whitgreaves sold all their land. The farm remained in use but was increasingly neglected. Wolverhampton Council bought it in 1978 and restored it in the 1980s.

DESCRIPTION
The original timber framed house is embedded in a larger brick built structure, of which Bay 1 has been destroyed and replaced. It is a variation on the very wide spread "lobby entrance" type of house found in England and transported to New England in the USA. The front door opened into a small lobby with a staircase leading to the bedrooms. A parlour lay to one side of the lobby and a kitchen to the other. In greater detail the house shows unique features, but investigations into these is incomplete. This farmhouse is not as spectacular an example of timber framing as other yeoman country houses in this book, such as the Oak House or Ford Green Farm, but it is interesting, and with the surrounding working farm and park particularly appealing to families with young children.

Oak House

WHERE
Map reference SP 998909; in Oak Road, West Bromwich, a short distance from the High Street. It is 1 mile north-west of Junction 1 of the M5.

TRANSPORT
Buses pass; enquiries 0121 200 2700. The nearest railway station is Dudley & Sandwell; enquiries 0121 643 2711.

ACCESS & FACILITIES
Owned by Sandwell Borough Council; for information on hours of opening phone 0121 553 0759 or 0121 556 0683.

HISTORY
The Oak House is a remarkable half timbered yeoman's house which stands incongruously in the urban jumble of the Black Country town of West Bromwich.

Oak House, West Bromwich

(70)

Yeoman families usually left few written records, and this is so for the Oak House. It is not certain who built it, but the most likely candidates were a family called Turton. They were prosperously middle class for the time; too insignificant to play a political role in the life of the area but having enough money from owning a few hundred acres of land to become involved in small local industries. The Oak House was probably built late in the reign of Elizabeth I and provides a particularly good example of the house of such a family.

Thomas Turton owned the house in 1634 and a deed records its sale to his younger brother John for £350. The Turtons were involved in the early metal industries of the Black Country. A William Turton (died 1628) bought two water mills in 1583; by 1610 one was producing blades. The family were also nailers and the family's increased wealth enabled them to extend the original house by adding brick extensions and the tower or belvedere, which is its most unusual feature.

By 1642 the Turtons had ceased calling themselves "yeomen" and become "gentlemen". However the family never rose to the ranks of the gentry. John Turton who owned the house during the Civil War occupied himself as steward of several local landowners and in money lending, neither of which were genteel activities. The house remained that of yeomen, albeit prosperous yeomen. It remained a notable local landmark in the 18th century, and in 1774 John Wesley preached in the courtyard. The Turton family ceased to live there in 1837 and the house was let and sub-let to tenants.

By the late Victorian period it was decayed and well on the way to demolition, as had happened to most such houses. But the rarity value of the Oak House was its salvation. In 1877 a national magazine, *The Building News,* ran an article about it. Learning of its importance a local figure, Alderman Rueben Farley, bought and restored the house, then donated it to the people of West Bromwich.

DESCRIPTION
The Oak House has two storeys and a big attic with an odd timber framed tower (or belvedere) in the centre. Legend has it that during the Civil War, Parliamentary soldiers were billeted in the casernes, or roof spaces, which were enlarged in the early 17th century, and used the belvedere as a lookout post. Certainly the Turtons supported Parliament, and the belvedere would give useful observation of the Royalists in Dudley Castle.

A good guide to the house is provided by the inventory of John Turton in 1705. The ground floor consisted of the parlour and inner parlour, hall, kitchen, bolting house and dairy, because the house produced its own cheese, butter and preserves from its farm. The inventory mentions crop stores, a variety of livestock, horses, farm implements and a shed and stable close by. None of these are recreated today, though a small 17th century barn stands on site. On the first floor were four bedrooms for the family, with a maids chamber, mens' chamber (both for servants), cheese chamber and an unnamed room. There seems to have been a study on the second floor. The house brewed its own beer, as was normal for its period, and in the cellar were several barrels, brewing vessels and an old brass furnace.

The Oak House has been furnished by the local council in the style of a 17th century yeoman's house. The furniture is on loan from the Victoria and Albert Museum and gives a good impression of the house as the Turtons would have known it.

Old Hall Gatehouse

WHERE
Map reference SK 082169; is next to the parish church in Mavesyn Ridware, 2.5 miles east of Rugeley.

TRANSPORT
Buses pass; enquiries 01785 223344.

ACCESS & FACILITIES
The Gatehouse is the private property of the owner of the Hall on whose land it stands, Mr Mark Eades. You can only obtain access by contacting him on 01543 490312. There are no WCs or refreshments.

HISTORY
In the lawless middle ages gatehouses were an important part of an estate, when a high wall and a well guarded entrance were vital to security. Very few survived the more peaceful conditions of post Tudor England, though some Tudor Gatehouses remain more because of their decorative than their defensive qualities. Mediaeval gatehouses are so rare that they are of great interest and this one is such a survival.

The Gatehouse has been dated at c1391, meaning that it was built by the Sir Robert Mavesyn who was involved in the famed mortal combat with Sir William Handsacre before the battle of Shrews-bury in 1403. [See the section *Five Centuries of Evolution*] The shape and site of the manor house of which the Gatehouse was part are unknown. It is likely to have been a quadrangle round a court-yard, with the entrance through the Gatehouse. At some point in the early to mid 16th century the building was encased in brick and stone to give its present appearance. By 1660 the manor house was in ruins, and it is not clear why the Gatehouse did not share its fate; it may have survived because the upper room could be used for storage or meetings.

In 1718 a Charles Chadwick demolished the old manor house and built a fair sized Georgian structure as a summer residence. He seems to have kept the Gatehouse as stabling or servants quarters. The estate passed through many changes of fortunes, and by the early 20th century the Hall was used as a farm and the gatehouse as a barn. That it survived is testimony to the strength of its cons-truction. Apart from occasional use for parish meetings it is now empty.

DESCRIPTION.
The Gatehouse is a half timbered structure partly covered by brick and stone from the 17th century. Its main feature is a large open room on the first floor where you can see the huge beams bracing the wall. There is evidence that one end of the room was made into a smaller unit at some point for use as a dovecote. The house is of considerable interest to the specialist.

Rowley's House

WHERE
The house is in Barker Street, in central Shrewsbury.

TRANSPORT
Car parking is available nearby. The house is within walking distance of the railway station (timetable enquiries 0121 643 2700) and the town centre generally. For bus information phone 01743 253030.

ACCESS & FACILITIES
Owned by Shrewsbury & Atcham Borough Council. For details of opening and refreshments phone 01743 361196.

Rowley's House, Shrewsbury

HISTORY

Rowley's House is a splendid two storey half timbered building
in the centre of Shrewsbury onto which is built a small Georgian
town house known as Rowley's Mansion. It was saved from
demolition in the 1930s and turned into a museum in 1972 by
Shrewsbury District Council.

The Rowleys were an old Shropshire merchant family, William
de Roulowe being recorded on a Guild Merchant Roll of 1252.
They were established maltsters and brewers by the time William
Rowley, (born 1572) extended the family interests from a farm
at Worfield to Shrewsbury. In 1594 William was recorded as a
Burgess of Shrewsbury. A lease from the Merchant Drapers
Company of this time refers to "One great tenement and two
cottages...let to William Rowley". The tenement was almost
certainly the timber framed Rowley's House, which has signs
of being a commercial rather than a domestic building. There
are no chimneys or fireplaces and a large sack hoist is built
into the roof timbers. When Rowley came to Shrewsbury he
may have lived on the site of the adjacent Rowley's Mansion.

This is a brick house, which he built in 1616-18 next to the timber framed building which he occupied with his family and servants.

He was probably using the House for brewing, as in 1635 there is a reference to a brewhouse, "the brewing vessels of which are capable of 100 measures". William became a prosperous merchant, moving into drapery in 1634 and becoming Master of the Shrewsbury Drapers in 1640. The property passed out of the family by marriage in the late 17th century to John Hill, husband of William's grandaughter Priscilla. For many years the brick building was known as Hill's Mansion before reverting to the title Rowley's Mansion. By the 18th century it was let to Thomas Adams, a local vicar who entertained Dr Johnson there in 1774. Later the area deteriorated but the house was saved and restored by the Borough Surveyor, A W Ward, in the 1930s.

DESCRIPTION
The Georgian brick Mansion and the timber framed House are now a local museum, particularly noted for the nationally important display of Roman items from Viroconium (Wroxeter) five miles away. The remains of the showpiece ceiling of the reception room of Rowley's Mansion looks down on tiles and pottery from the Ironbridge Gorge area. Most of the exhibits are of a general nature, but The Rowley Room displays a bed of the late Elizabethan period, set among portraits and other objects to reveal something of the life of Rowley's Mansion.

Sandon Hall, Staffordshire

Sandon Hall

WHERE
Map reference SJ 954297; 4 miles north-east of Stafford on the A51
between Stone and Rugeley.

TRANSPORT
Buses pass; enquiries 01785 223344.

ACCESS & FACILITIES
Sandon Hall is owned by the Harrowby family and not usually open
to the public. However, special arrangements are made for parties
and the Hall is occasionally open for special events. Get details of
opening times, admission charges, etc from Michael Bosson on
01889 508004.

HISTORY
Sandon Hall is one of the few great Staffordshire houses still lived
in by the family who built it. The Harrowby's were a major influence
on the liberal wing of the Tory party in the 18th and 19th centuries,
and their house reflects the life of a wealthy but high minded family
of that period.

The estate lies on a ridge overlooking the Trent Valley, and has
been a seat of the Ryders for over two centuries. The family fortune
was made by Sir Dudley Ryder, a lawyer who became Lord Chief
Justice in 1754. His country seat was in Grantham, and it was his
son Nathaniel (1735 to 1803) who bought the Sandon estate in 1776.
Nathaniel was created Baron Harrowby and had three distinguished
sons, the eldest of whom became the 1st Earl of Harrowby and sat
in Parliament for fifty years. His eldest son Dudley followed this
tradition and was a member of the cabinet of Lord Liverpool, Wellington, Peel and Palmerston. He made prolonged visits to Italy in
the second quarter of the 19th century and built a substantial
cultural collection. The 3rd Earl, also named Dudley, sat for the
family seat of Tiverton and was President of the British & Foreign
Bible Society. The family met the agricultural depression of the
late 19th century by diversifying into banking, and the 5th Earl,
John Herbert Dudley, was a partner of Coutts Bank and an MP.
The 6th Earl, the present Earl's father, was a noted historian.

The Ryders were thus at the centre of English political, academic,
cultural and religious life for over two centuries. They married into
the wealthiest and most opulent circles in the land, including the

landed wealth of the Levenson-Gower family (the Sutherlands) and the Coutts banking family. In the 18th and 19th centuries they built houses which reflected their growing wealth and status. The building bought by the Ryders in 1776 was of stone and designed by Joseph Pickford of Derby. This house, altered by Samuel Wyatt, was badly damaged by fire in June 1848. A new design was commissioned from William Burns who provided a house in the Victorian version of the Jacobean style. It is this house in fine 18th century parkland which survives today.

DESCRIPTION
The building is a two storey house of ashlar stone in nine bays. The entrance front has a porte cochere and small turrets either side of gables shaped in the Jacobean style. The design is restrained and avoids Victorian excesses.

The interior includes a grand Inner Hall or Saloon, surrounded by a series of fine state rooms and an impressive conservatory. While the house is fully Victorian, the furnishings and pictures are not. When the fire of 1848 took place the servants and local railway workers salvaged most of the contents, even down to Wyatt's chimneys and plate glass windows. After re-building, these items were augmented by good Victorian furniture. The collection has remained largely unaltered to the present day.

The house has a museum telling the family history, including costumes, toys, the imitation duelling pistols of Prime Minister William Pitt the Younger, an entire room decorated with hand painted Chinese wallpaper, and a unique collection of World War I posters. The 50 acre garden is landscaped and noted for its azaleas and rhododendrons. The Parkland is a fine example of 18th century landscape, with interesting monuments to our only murdered Prime Minister, Spencer Perceval c1812, a column monument to Pitt from 1806, and the top tower of Trentham Hall which was bought when that house was demolished in 1912.

The Church of All Saints stands three quarters of a mile from the house on the edge of the Park. It is worth visiting for the remarkable monument of 1603 to the historian Sampson Erdeswick, a recumbent figure flanked by two kneeling wives between two columns. Built in 1601 before Erdeswick died, it is one of the finest examples of its kind anywhere and a startling tribute to the egoism of a man who presents himself as being worshipped by *two* spouses.

Shipton Hall

Map reference SJ 563919; in Shipton, 6.5 miles south-west of Much Wenlock on the B4378 near the junction with the B4368 to Morville and Bridgnorth.

TRANSPORT
Buses pass, though not often; enquiries 01743 253030.

ACCESS & FACILITIES
Shipton Hall is privately owned and details of the opening hours can be obtained on 01746 785225. Parties of twenty or more are welcome throughout the year by appointment; refreshments and buffet meals can be provided for them.

HISTORY
Shipton Hall is a striking, stone Elizabethan house of the 1580s facing the Much Wenlock - Craven Arms road in Shropshire's remote and beautiful Corvedale. It lies on rising ground flanked by lawns and trees. There is an ancient church to the south and Georgian stables to the east. Architecturally it is similar to nearby Wilderhope Manor and Weston Hall east of Stafford, but with the addition of a tower. Unusually, it is only partly Elizabethan, for the house was Georgianised and extended around 1760. Unlike Morville Hall 8 miles to the east, the Georgian owners left the Elizabethan facade intact, presumably appreciating its charm.

The site is ancient and the church dates back to Saxon times. A house certainly stood here in the early Tudor period, but this was a half timbered building destroyed by fire in 1549. The present house was built in the local limestone by Richard Lutwyche around 1587. If this date is correct, it is a remarkable coincidence that a very similar limestone manor house was being built a mile away at Wilderhope at the same time, Wilderhope is dated at 1586, and that both have survived. Presumably the builders of the two houses learned from each other. Lutwyche lived at the neighbouring Lutwyche Hall, and it is said that he gave Shipton as a dowry when his daughter Elizabeth married Thomas Mytton. If so it is again fascinating that the very similar Weston Hall is also rumoured to be a Dower House. The house remained in the Mytton family for 300 years. Nothing of great historical significance took place at Shipton, and it appears to be typical of the vast majority of gentry houses where a life of leisure and affluence was lived quietly and to the full.

DESCRIPTION

The house has been described as "an exquisite specimen of Elizabethan architecture set in a quaint, old fashioned garden, the whole
forming a picture which ... satisfies the artistic sense of even the
most fastidious". This is exactly right. The three triangular gables
flank a tower rising to the height of the star shaped brick chimney
stacks to make a most pleasing asymmetrical pattern. It is fortunate
that when the Georgian owners modernised the interior and doubled
the size of the house by extensions, they left the facade intact.

Inside the house there is an interesting combination of elegant
Georgian roccoco decor with fine Tudor and Jacobean panelling
and timberwork. You can see how the old timbered house was
incorporated into the new stone house built around it. Many of
the mediaeval timbers and some doors survive. Items of particular
interest include the plasterwork of the ceilings and chimney pieces,
some of which are by Thomas F Pritchard. Pritchard (died 1778)
was an engineer and architect best known for designing the Iron
Bridge over the Severn. He built five houses, including Hatton
Grange near Shifnal, and designed the Georgian extension at
Shipton. The panelling of the bedrooms and the old Solar are
from the 16th and early 17th centuries. Some of the original
leaded diamond panes remain intact.

In the grounds, the dominant feature is an elegant Georgian stable
block of nine bays topped by a cupola. Behind it lies a dovecote,
possibly 13th century, indicating the status of the original manor
house, since they could only be granted to Lords of the Manor by
Royal Charter. The small parish church to the east is Norman,
especially the nave, with little of the Saxon original. The chancel
was rebuilt in 1589 by John, youngest son of Richard Lutwyche.
There are interesting monuments to the Mytton family.

Shugborough, Staffordshire

Shugborough

WHERE
Map reference SJ 993225. The main entrance is at Milford, 3.5 miles east of Stafford on the A513. There is a second entrance from Great Haywood off the A51 which gives access (on foot only) over the mediaeval Essex Bridge.

TRANSPORT
Buses pass frequently on the A513; enquiries 01785 223344. The main entrance is 1.5 miles from the house and there is no transport. Cars pay parking charges. Buses also pass through Great Haywood but sparsely. Parking here is very limited

ACCESS & FACILITIES
This is a National Trust property which is still partly occupied by its former owner, Lord Lichfield, and by the Staffordshire County Museum. In the grounds is a model farm. Access to the grounds is free, otherwise charges vary depending on what you want to see, and National Trust members have free admission only to the house. Get details of opening times and charges from 01889 881388. The house and model farm have tea rooms and WCs. There is an excellent cafe near the attractive canal lock at the Great Haywood entrance - which also provides limited free parking for customers.

HISTORY
Shugborough is the product of the enterprise of the Anson family. Their current representative is the photographer Patrick Lichfield, Earl of Lichfield and cousin to the Queen, who still lives here. However the survival and prosperity of the house and its 900 acre estate depends on an unusual and welcome alliance between Staffordshire County Council, which runs the house and farm as the County Museum, and the National Trust. The mansion house is magnificent and the working farm of great importance in the history of British agriculture, but the outstanding feature of the estate is the Parkland. Pevsner remarks "For picturesque grounds and garden furnishings few houses in England can compete with Shugborough. The approach from the Milford Lodges will never be forgotten".

Shugborough is a Georgian success story. The original building was a small squire's house overshadowed by nearby Ingestre Hall, Tixall Hall and the Beaudesert home of the Pagets. Its rise to become a house of national importance was due to Thomas Anson and still more to his younger brother, George. Thomas inherited the house in 1720 to become the Squire. George joined the Navy and became one of the great admirals in British history. He was the second British commander (after Drake) to circumnavigate the globe, which he did in 1740-44. On the way he captured a Spanish treasure galleon which made his fortune.

George Anson made over much of his fortune to his elder brother to develop the family seat. Thomas had inherited a two storey brick house built by his father in 1695 with 80 acres of land, and had started to buy land around Shugborough before his brother's fortune became available. With the money came ambitious plans. Thomas bought over 1000 acres of land, removed the ancient village in front of the house to nearby Haywood and created a model landscape. The old millpond was converted into a small lake with a mock chinese pagoda at one end, the stream in front of the house was culverted and roads diverted or destroyed.

When George died without issue in 1762, having risen to First Lord of the Admiralty, all his fortune came to his brother. Thomas immediately employed the pioneer of Greek revival architect, James "Athenian" Stuart, to erect the remarkable series of imitation Greek monuments which make Shugborough one of the most important examples of the genre in Britain. The Ansons treated the Park partly as an ornamental playground, with the women dressing up as Shepherdesses. However they also farmed seriously, using the latest developments of the agrarian revolution to develop a commercially valuable estate.

The increasing funds available to Thomas were also put into the house. By 1748 two new wings had been added to the 17th century main block, and an extra storey was added in 1768. Thomas also collected paintings, but most of his old masters were sold in 1842. His death unmarried led to his nephew Thomas Anson II (Viscount Anson) inheriting in 1789. The Viscount brought in the architect Samuel Wyatt to rebuild and enlarge the house in the neo-classical style, and this work was done between 1790 and 1806 to create the house we see today. Wyatt not only extended Shugborough; he tried to unify the facade by erecting a large Ionic porch without pediment covering the full width and upper two storeys of the centre block.

From 1795 the Viscount applied the new methods of the agrarian revolution with a ruthlessness which astonished contemporaries. The line of the main Stafford - Lichfield road was diverted west over Cannock Chase. Between 1800 and 1806 the remnants of the village clustering near the Tower of the Winds were swept away. It was replaced by a model farm with the dairy in the Tower, a good example of how Viscount Anson transformed the decorative elements of his inheritance to commercial use. At the White Barn a further complex of farm buildings was erected which housed the first stationary, water driven threshing machine in Staffordshire. The walled kitchen garden had a steam heated hothouse where melons and cucumbers could be grown at any time of the year.

Anson was emulating the improvements of his father in law, the famous agricultural improver Coke of Holkham. His work makes Shugborough as important in the history of agrarian improvement as its architectural and classical features. By the time he had finished, Anson's estate spread over 2,000 acres, with 100 head of cattle and 1,700 sheep; it was farmed as efficiently as any in the world.

Alas this splendid estate was wasted by his son and heir. Thomas William Anson spent a fortune in the corrupt politics of the time, bribing enough voters to become MP for Lichfield. He spent even more money buying land near Ranton Abbey west of Stafford and making it into one of the finest sporting estates in the country. A painting of 1840, *A Shooting Party at Ranton Abbey,* featuring the Prime Minister Melbourne, still hangs in Shugborough. But it was addiction to the turf which ruined the 1st Earl. In 1842 he had to sell the contents of Shugborough and his London home to pay his debts. Today only a book, three or four paintings and a few pieces of sculpture remain of Thomas Anson's magnificent collections.

The 2nd Earl inherited in 1854 and slowly began to revive Shugborough, which was closed and empty for twelve years. However the estate was badly hit by the agrarian depression of the 1880s, and the 3rd Earl (who inherited in 1892) could only restore it by overseas investments and becoming a director of several city companies. As his fortune recovered, he renovated the house in the Georgian style, thus avoiding the excesses of Victoriana. When the 4th Earl inherited in 1918 Shugborough was a going concern, and he avoided the interwar problems which destroyed other houses such as nearby Beaudesert. Unlike Alton Towers, the house avoided serious damage during the War despite a large army camp in the grounds. On the death of the 4th Earl in 1960 the estate was given to the National Trust in part payment of death duties. They could not meet the cost of maintaining so complex an estate, and the County Council stepped in to take over the lease in association with the Trust. The 4th Earl was succeeded by his grandson, Patrick Lichfield, who has become a leading photographer and still lives in the private parts of the house with his three children.

DESCRIPTION

No brief description can do justice to Shugborough, an estate of three distinct parts. The house is a classic mansion with a rich treasure of painting, sculpture, furniture and decor which rivals all but the greatest houses in the country. The guide book deals comprehensively with the contents of the stately portions of the house. The Grade I gardens nearby can be seen without paying the entrance fee, except for the private parts for which you need permission. The park is one of the most important landscapes of any country house in Britain, and the farm is nearly as important in the history of farming. The apparently timeless rustic landscape is the product of meticulous planning, for both a major canal and railway run through the estate less than a mile from the house, yet neither are obtrusive, with the main Euston to Glasgow line almost totally buried in a deep cutting.

What Pevsner calls the "garden furnishings" have to be seen to be believed. Visitors enter the park from Milford through restrained wrought iron gates between the two Stafford Lodges. These tiny, square, classical houses have plain columns, medallions and niches, making grand looking lodgings for estate staff. Further on and surrounded by woodland is the polyagonal Stafford Wood Lodge, then in the open parkland you meet the Lantern of Diogenes; very Greek with a bowl and black dolphins. The Arch of Hadrian stands triumphantly on a small hill commemorating the Admiral's famous voyage and carries busts and the tombs of the great man and his wife. The Tower of the Winds is an octagonal, two storied tower with classical porches on two sides. The ground floor is still equipped as the farm dairy. Later on you will see the Doric Temple which is just a six columned portico fronting a sort of brick shed. However, it is the earliest classical monument in Britain after a similar job at Hagley Hall. There is a Chinese House and much later Chinese Bridge in cast iron. More astonishing, a monster urn on a huge pedestal turns out to be a monument to one of the Anson cats. The Shepherd's Monument has fancy columns and a frieze. Trent Lodge is an Italianate house by Essex Bridge. Even the railway has a classical tunnel portal and a bridge.

The visitor to Shugborough will see a historic estate whose richness it is hard to appreciate. Its development and survival to the present day is a classic example of an aristocratic estate growing from humble beginnings through the commercial and agrarian revolutions of the 18th century.

Sudbury Hall

WHERE
Map reference SK 155321; in Sudbury Village, 6 miles east of Uttox-
eter on the A50.

TRANSPORT
Buses pass; enquiries 01785 223344.

ACCESS & FACILITIES
A National Trust house; get details of opening hours and admission
charges on 01283 585305. The house features a Museum of Child-
hood. Light lunches and teas are served in the coach house.

HISTORY
Sudbury Hall is a magnificent but puzzling mansion on the Staffordshire - Derbyshire border which was built in the last forty years
of the 17th century by one man, George Vernon. He was a wealthy
Derbyshire squire and apparently his own architect, but his career
and methods are strangely obscure given the size and splendour of
the house. It is curiously difficult to understand how Vernon built
a mansion of such splendour while leaving so few records. Sudbury
is a blend of styles that were old fashioned when Vernon came to
build it, beside the most up to date innovations of his day. Almost
untouched since Vernon died in 1702, the house is a time capsule
of late Stuart splendour, and the more pleasing because of its many
idiosyncracies. The result is a puzzle and a delight.

The origins of Sudbury Hall are mysterious; it is not even certain
that George Vernon started building it. There are obvious Jacobean
influences on the exterior, notably the diapered (ornamental criss
cross) brickwork which is also found at Aston Hall, carved stone
ornaments, variously coloured brickwork and oddly old fashioned
windows. These suggest that the building was started before the
Civil War. It is widely believed that Vernon completed a building
started by his grandmother but interrupted by the War. However
latest research suggests that Mary Vernon lived in a small manor
house which was demolished to make way for the present Hall.
The old fashioned elements of the design may be explained by the
relative remoteness of the area in the 1660s. George Vernon may
simply have been out of touch with Restoration fashion, but as he
built his house over forty years learnt more and more about the
latest developments. So while the exterior is old fashioned, the
interior saw the best craftsmen, notably Grinling Gibbons.

The scanty evidence suggests that Vernon began building his house in 1659, designing it himself with the advice of local craftsmen. The shell took five years to complete, but the interior twenty. The plan and much of the detail of the walls was old fashioned by the 1660s, but the hipped roof and central cupola with golden ball reflecting the sun's rays are almost the hallmark of architecture in Charles II's time. The massive chimney stacks are Jacobean, but their design suggests knowledge of Clarendon House, London, supporting the theory that George Vernon picked up new ideas as work progressed.

In the 1670s Vernon replaced the local men who had started the work. Samuel Mansfield, plasterer, and William Wilson, the carver responsible for the stone frontispieces on front and back were dismissed. In their place came the finest London experts of the day - Robert Bradbury and James Pettifer, plasterers, and Edward Pierce and Grinling Gibbons, carvers. In the 1690s Vernon took on Thomas Young, who went to work at Chatsworth, and Louis Laguerre, who worked at Chatsworth from 1689 to 1694. Vernon undoubtedly knew of the new Baroque house the Devonshires were erecting at Chatsworth and is presumed to be making an attempt to bring the decor up to date. Fortunately this had a marginal influence. Whilst Ham House in London is the most complete Charles II house in terms of furniture and fabrics, Sudbury is by far the most complete in terms of decoration.

After Vernon's death in 1702 the house was little altered. The main changes were the replacement of the original balustrade crowning the roof with a stone one which rises above the cornice. The architect Anthony Salvin carried out some tactful interior changes in the 19th century, but luckily his plan of 1837 to turn the house into a Gothic monstrosity was stillborn. A modest service wing was instead added to the east. On the whole, if George Vernon returned today he would recognise his house. When it was given to the National Trust in 1967 Sudbury Hall was clearly a major Carolingian survival, and was superbly restored as such between 1968 and 1970.

By contrast, the garden has been much altered. The original formal garden laid out by George Vernon was destroyed by his grandson, the 1st Lord Vernon, who "naturalised" the landscape in the manner of Capability Brown. The garden was further remodelled by the 5th Lord Vernon in the 1830s, enhancing the picturesque qualities of the grounds by enlarging the lake and creating an island, but with formal flower beds reintroduced on the south side of the house. In 1970 the National Trust made two star shaped borders and planted topiary plants on other terraces and paths.

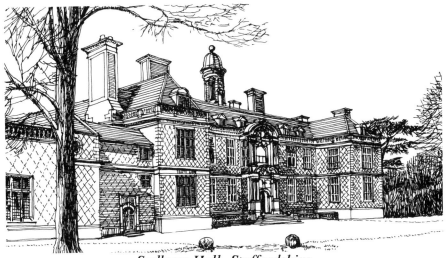

Sudbury Hall, Staffordshire

DESCRIPTION

The exterior of Sudbury Hall is heavy, dull and forbidding and will interest only a few experts. It totally belies the richness and splendour of the interior, which is both exceptionally interesting to professionals and an abiding source of pleasure to everyone else. The decor and furnishings are so rich that no short description would be adequate. It is often suggested that the twenty years of the Civil War repressed the energies of the aristocratic and gentry classes, which burst out in an exuberance of creativity with the Restoration of the monarchy. Sudbury gives considerable weight to the theory.

We can only note a few of the treasures. The staircase has been called "perhaps the finest staircase of its date in situ in an English country house", and the work of Edward Pierce in carving the balustrade, "deserves to be ranked among the carver's finest achievements". High praise, given that Pierce worked on six of Wren's churches. Equally noteworthy is the Long Gallery, old fashioned by the 1660s but with a ceiling by Robert Bradbury that has been described as "perhaps the finest of its kind in any English House". The plasterwork by Bradbury and Pettifer is superb. However it is more than matched by the work of Grinling Gibbons whose drawing room chimneypiece carving of 1678 is remarkable.

The Staffordshire - Derbyshire border was a backwater three centuries ago when George Vernon built his house. Perhaps its survival owes something to the relative isolation of the area even today. It is a mixed blessing that isolation has also left the house in relative obscurity, because it deserves to be better known.

Trentham Gardens

WHERE
Map reference SJ 862415; by the A34 Newcastle under Lyme to
Stafford road at the Trentham roundabout, and midway between
that road and the M6.

TRANSPORT
Buses pass frequently; enquiries 01785 223344.

ACCESS & FACILITIES
Trentham Gardens has long been owned by British Coal, but as we
go to press they are disposing of it to we know not who. However,
we understand that you can still get details of opening hours,
admission charges and facilities on 01782 657341.

HISTORY
This book does not deal with the vanished houses of Shropshire and
Staffordshire, such as Beaudesert or Wolseley. However Trentham
is exceptional, because while the house has gone, many of the out-
buildings remain in a Capability Brown Park of great importance.
In recent years the estate has deteriorated into a shabby leisure
facility, but there are plans afoot which may lead to its revival.

Trentham was part of one of the most important and controversial
aristocratic estates in Britain - that of the Dukes of Sutherland. The
1st Duke was George Granville Leveson Gower, of a family which
grew rich by acquiring lands in Staffordshire and Shropshire after
the Reformation. In 1803 Leveson-Gower inherited a manor house at
Trentham set in a Capability Brown landscape, plus the title Marquis
of Stafford. More important, he had married the Countess of Sutherland who brought him huge estates in the Scottish Highlands. Leveson-
Gower owned more acres than anyone else in Britain, and set about
maximising his returns by evicting his Highland tenants to replace
them with more profitable sheep. The Highland clearances were little
short of "ethnic cleansing", but this did not trouble the Marquis or
his fellow aristocrats. In the last year of his life, he was created 1st
Duke of Sutherland, and it is his imperious statue which you can see
on the A34 staring down at Trentham.

The 2nd Duke and his wife inherited the estate in 1833 and employed
Sir Charles Barry, designer of the Houses of Parliament, to rebuild
their old manor house on the newest lines. The result made Barry's
reputation. He built a huge new house in an Italian villa style then

almost unknown in Britain, but *cf* Cronkhill at Attingham. With the attached sculpture gallery, clock tower and stables to match it was enormously successful. The style became madly popular, and appears in Queen Victoria's house at Osborne, many Victorian houses in town and country and innumerable water pumping stations.

Alas for the house, it did not last eighty years. Pollution from industrial Stoke on Trent made the River Trent foul, and by the start of the 20th century the Capability Brown lake had to be fed from other sources. The river flowed within a hundred yards of the house, and by 1912 the smell had driven out the Sutherlands. It is not so good today. No one would buy so large a building, so it was demolished and the Capability Brown landscape given to the City of Stoke on Trent. For many years the grounds belonged to the Coal Board, *aka* British Coal, and are seriously neglected. The land lies within the boundaries of Staffordshire County Council and Stafford Borough Council who are currently proposing a to designate it as a Conservation Area.

Trentham Gardens, Stoke on Trent

DESCRIPTION

The house has gone, but the sculpture gallery and stables with their fine clock tower remain, along with Charles Barry's Gothic style church and some small, free standing pavilions. The grounds are now a scruffy leisure park with Jet-skiing on the Capability Brown lake. The statue of the 1st Duke on a hill overlooking the grounds is badly vandalised and overgrown. The Sutherland Mausoleum across the A34 is neglected and the graves around it astonishingly affected by mining subsidence; in the light of the family's history it is tempting to speculate where their occupants might have gone. After demolition the top tower of Barry's building was moved to Sandon Hall but it too has been neglected and is in a very poor condition. The estate deserves better than this and it is hoped that the local councils can rescue it.

Upton Cresset Hall

WHERE
Map reference SK 655925; 2 miles up a single track road off the
B4364 Bridgnorth - Ludlow Road, and 4 miles west of Bridgnorth.

TRANSPORT
Buses pass on the A458 and less frequently on the the B4364, but
you will have to make your own way for the last 2 miles to the
house. Enquiries - 01743 253030.

ACCESS & FACILITIES
Upton Cressett Hall is a private home which is normally open to the
public on Thursday afternoons from spring to autumn. Get details of
opening hours and admission prices on 01746 714307. Self catering
accommodation is available in the Gatehouse. Refreshments are not
usually provided, but arrangements for pre-booked parties and
individuals may be possible.

HISTORY
Upton Cressett is a mediaeval manor house rebuilt in the Tudor
period, which stands in a remote part of Shropshire. Although now
very much a 20th century home, the quaint antiquity of the Tudor
buildings framed by trees, the remains of a mediaeval moat and the
little 12th century church create a distinct sense of stepping back
into the past.

The Manor of Upton Cressett was the ancient home of the de Upton
and Cressett families. By intermarriage they held their estate in
unbroken succession from the Norman Conquest to the 20th century.
The family played a leading role in Shropshire and national life from
the 13th to the 18th centuries. Thomas Cressett was imprisoned in the
Marshalsea, probably for conspiracy, but was pardoned in 1505 and
reconciled to the Tudor throne. In 1512 he supplied troops for Henry
VIII. Richard Cressett built the Gatehouse in the reign of Elizabeth,
and encased the mediaeval manor house in brick in 1580. In 1588 he
made the second largest Shropshire contribution to the Armada fund.

Richard's son Edward was a Royalist who was killed at the Battle of
Bridgnorth in 1646. One of his sons was Treasurer and Steward to
Charles I. The family continued to be of national importance under
the Hanoverians. Edward's grandson James was envoy extraordinary
to the Court of Hanover under William and Mary and Queen Anne,
and played a significant role in securing the Hanoverian succession.

Another descendant of Edward, James Cressett, was confidante and secretary to Augusta, Dowager Princess of Wales. Thereafter the family ceased to be of national importance. In the 20th century the house, then dilapidated, was bought by Mr and Mrs William Cash who restored it.

DESCRIPTION
Upton Cressett Hall is a good example of the house of a squire or upper gentry family of the late mediaeval and early modern era. It was originally encircled by a water filled moat with a drawbridge between the Hall and the Gatehouse. Half of the moat can still be seen to the north of the Hall. In the woods and fields nearby there are earthworks indicating mediaeval fishponds and a mediaeval village.

Inside the house, the entrance lets into the lower part of the 14th century Great Hall. This is now the dining room and displays the vertical timbers of the Great Hall. It contains a Jacobean chest and cross banded, draw leaf refectory table. Leading to the right is the drawing room, with Elizabethan panelling and fireplace. Behind the fireplace is a secret door which might have led via a hidden passageway to the upper part of the house and a tunnel to the Gatehouse. In the kitchen is a 13 foot wide fireplace with a timber framed wall which was part of the original exterior of the 14th century house.

Upstairs, visitors can see the upper part of the Great Hall, now a bedroom, which was constructed in the 14th century. The massive timbers form an arch 14 feet across. To the left of the Great Hall is a cross wing built in the early and later parts of the 15th century.

At the front of the house is the striking 16th century Gatehouse. It is most pleasantly idiosyncratic, with two octangular turrets on either side of the small central archway, and twentysix transomed windows. On the first floor you can see the treasure of the Hall, exceptional plasterwork ceilings and a plasterwork overmantel. The motifs include a Tudor rose, portcullis and Beaufort feathers, and the execution is so similar to that at nearby Wilderhope and Moreville that the same craftsmen must have been responsible. From the second floor there are panoramic views of the countryside, the Hall and the 12th century Norman church.

Weston Hall

WHERE
Map reference SJ 965270; by the River Trent and .5 mile west of
Weston where the A518 crosses the A51.

TRANSPORT
Buses pass; enquiries 01785 223344.

ACCESS & FACILITIES
Weston Hall is privately owned and not open to the public because
the dilapidated building is being converted into a hotel. The
ground floor will become a bar and restaurant and is planned to
open in 1996. Information can be obtained from 01785 48111.

HISTORY
Weston Hall is the most enigmatic property in this book. It is a fine
stone house which faces the village of Weston, but even less is known
about it than about the Ancient High House in Stafford. The current
owner is Stafford businessman Paul Reynolds, who believes that the
main block was built around 1550, though the architectural evidence
suggests it is late Elizabethan.

There is a remarkable lack of documentary evidence about Weston
Hall. Paul Reynolds believes it was originally built as a small dower
house around 1550, then enlarged in about 1660 into a three gable
structure with high pitched roofs. While England enjoyed a house
building boom after the restoration in 1660, it is unlikely that the
Hall would at that time have been enlarged in late Tudor style. The
three frontal bays are of Elizabethan appearance, very similar to
the buildings at Shipton and Wilderhope in Shropshire which were
built in the 1580s. If the main block was built around 1660, this
style was being used eighty years after its heyday.

Towards the end of the 19th century the house was taken over by
the Shrewsbury Settled Estates. In about 1900 they made further
extensions in Elizabethan style, built a fourth frontage and raised
the main entrance to the first floor. In 1904 the Hall was leased to
Staffordshire County Council for use as a lunatic asylum, but it
remained in the hands of the Estates until 1950, when the Godwin
family bought and converted it into flats. By the early 1990s the
Hall was in a poor structural state and derelict. At that point Paul
Reynolds bought the building and secured the fabric. His convert-
ion work shows admirable respect for its antiquity.

Weston Hall, Staffordshire

Weston Park, Staffordshire

Weston Park

Map reference SJ 807107; at Weston under Lizard on the A5 midway between Telford and Cannock. It is about 8 miles west of the
M6 Junction 12 and 2.5 miles north of the M54 Junction 3.

TRANSPORT
No buses.

ACCESS & FACILITIES
Weston Park is privately owned but regularly open to the public.
For information on opening hours for the Park and house, and entry
charges phone 01952 850207. There are WCs and plenty of parking
space. The house has a tea room and bar.

HISTORY
Weston Park is a classic stately home in extensive grounds. It was
built in 1671 and is an example of the revival in architecture after
the monarchy was restored. The Park was landscaped by Capability
Brown and contains fine wooded pleasure grounds with features
designed by James Paine. It may remind you of nearby Chillington.
Next to the house is a splendid Victorian formal garden. Today the
estate is run on business lines with open air concerts at midsummer.
Weston therefore represents three centuries of development and is a
living, working estate which has adapted to change under the ownership of the Bradford family.

The present Earl of Bradford claims that the estate has been owned
by his family since the 12th century. This is true, but not in direct
line of descent. They can be traced back to the Domesday Book,
when the de Westons owned the land, but the male line ended
in 1350 and it passed to the Mytton family. The Park descended
through them until in 1638 it was left to Elizabeth Mytton, an
only daughter, who in 1651 married Sir Thomas Wilbraham.

Lady Wilbraham was a remarkable woman, one of the very few
in the history of English architecture to have emulated the famous
Bess of Hardwick and designed a major building. (This is still true
today.) Lady Wilbraham had the present house built, and her copy
of Palladio's *First Book of Architecture* of 1663 is still in the Library, with her notes and costings in the margin. She bore three
daughters, the eldest of whom in 1681 married Richard Newport,
2nd Earl of Bradford, thus bringing the house into the Newport

family. The estate passed through the Newport family until 1762, when the 4th Earl of Bradford of the first creation died. It then passed into the hands of the Bridgeman family in the person of Sir Henry Bridgeman of Castle Bromwich, the 4th Earl's nephew.

Sir Henry immediately made Weston his main seat, using his new fortune to establish himself as owner by hiring Capability Brown to redesign the landscape. He also brought in James Paine to build a Roman bridge on the Temple Pool and the Temple of Diana in the grounds. Much French furniture was bought as well as the Boucher-Neilson tapestries from the Gobelin factory. Sir Henry died in 1800 and was succeeded by his son, Orlando. He developed the farm side of the estate and by 1803 was working to the principles pioneered by Coke of Norfolk. Orlando was made the 1st Earl of Bradford of the second creation in 1815. The Bridgeman's were an important County family who played a considerable part in the political and sporting life of the nation. In 1892 the 3rd Earl won the Derby with his horse *Sir Hugo,* while in her old age his wife received some 1,100 letters from Disraeli. They are now kept in the Staffordshire Record Office.

The 3rd Earl enlarged and developed the house, building the orangery and loggia to enable the family to go to church in wet weather without a soaking. The 4th Earl was Conservative MP for North Shropshire from 1867 to 1885, and the family became one of the landed pillars of the Tory party. Before inheriting in 1915 the 5th Earl had been Private Secretary to two Conservative Prime Ministers, Salisbury and Balfour. The 6th Earl devoted himself to developing the estate, a tradition energetically maintained by the 7th Earl who inherited in 1981.

DESCRIPTION
The house is a big, red brick, three storey building with eleven bays on the park front; the exterior is not particularly attractive. However the interior is a classic example of wealth applied to create an elegant environment. It is now very much in 17th and 18th century mode because, Mary Montgomery, wife of the 6th Earl, made many improvements to relieve the house of some Victorian decorative excesses.

The rooms open to the public are mainly on the ground floor and designed to impress the visitor with elegance and high culture. The entrance and marble hall leading into the interior are littered with fine pictures, furniture and a fine porcelain collection in cabinets. The furniture and tapestries in the rooms near the entrance are of great interest, particularly the Gobelin works which dominate the Tapestry Room. The drawing room contains 17th century family portraits of which the most important is Lely's portrait of Lady Wilbraham, while the book lined study has a portrait of Sir Orlando Bridgeman, the father of Sir Henry Bridgeman, Keeper of the Great Seal. The bag which held this object been made into an ugly fireguard and stands in the library.

The Dining Room contains three Van Dycks, and from this point on the perambulation through the house is less a walk through a home than a visit to a cross between a museum and an art gallery. This will suit many visitors. In fact, the guidebook says so, stating that one of the main ideas behind much of recent alterations at Weston has been to provide a setting for the superb collection of pictures.

However, there is little sense of an environment designed to be lived in and for this you may find the gardens and pleasure grounds more attractive. Weston Park covers more than 1,000 acres surrounded by a wall 8 miles long, but the key elements for the visitor are the Formal Gardens and the Pleasure Grounds. The Formal Gardens on the Park side of the house were originally Victorian, and have been reconstructed from photographs of the period. You can pursue an expansive walk past the Italian Garden and Orangery, through the Deer Park and the Teardrop Garden to return back to the Church Pool and Old Stables behind the house. This is a delight for those interested in formal gardening.

An alternative walk for those more interested in Capablility Brown style artificial naturalism runs from the Old Stables and round the Temple Wood. James Paine's Temple of Diana and Roman Bridge of 1760 can be inspected at close quarters. Both the horticulturalist and the lover of landscape can find much to enjoy.

Whitmore Hall

WHERE
Map reference SJ 810414; 4 miles south-west of Newcastle under Lyme on the A53 by the Mainwaring Arms pub. WARNING. The crossroads is a notorious accident black spot. Take great care turning north onto the road to Keele.

TRANSPORT
Buses pass; enquiries 01785 223344.

ACCESS & FACILITIES

You can park in the grounds, but because of fast moving traffic on the A53 it is easier to park next to the Mainwaring Arms. Get information about opening hours and admission prices on 01782 680478. The house has no refreshments or WCs; both are available at the Mainwaring Arms and, when they are open, the nearby Whitmore Galleries Tea Rooms.

HISTORY

Whitmore Hall is an ancient, modest squire's house. It lies down a corridor of lime trees behind the church of St Mary and All Saints and is invisible from the road. The original house and the very odd stables to the north are Elizabethan, but it was modernised after the Restoration and now appears as Carolingian.

Whitmore has been held since the Norman Conquest by only five families: de Whitmore, de Verdon, de Boghay, Mainwaring, and Cavenagh. It has never been sold, but passed from generation to generation, the family name only changing when the house was inherited by a woman. The original of the present building was a timber framed structure which was fortified for Parliament in the Civil War. The then owner, Edward Mainwaring, carried out the destruction of nearby Heleigh Castle for Parliament in 1645. The guide book states that it was he who carried out the reconstruction of Whitmore in 1676. I suspect this is untrue since he would then have been 73, and more likely it was carried out by his son, also called Edward.

Whoever started the work, the front was encased in eighteen inches of red Flemish bonded brickwork with stone dressings. There are four storeys and at the front, where only two are apparent, nine bays. A new hipped roof was built at the same time, which was surrounded by a stone ballustraded parapet. The interior was re-built to produce larger but fewer rooms, the number of hearths being reduced from nineteen to fourteen. Two Corinthian columns were added in the entrance hall and the present staircase. The porch was added in 1842 incorporating re-set heraldic work and blank ovals from 1676.

The rear of the Hall remained half timbered until a fire in 1880 when it was rebuilt in brick. Overall, the Hall represents the type of squire's house typical of the wealthy but not opulent, gentry families which dominated rural England from the Conquest to the 19th century.

DESCRIPTION

Visitors approach the Hall on a road which winds beside the avenue of limes; that you can only negotiate on foot. It provides an excellent perspective of the front, albeit not quite symmetrical. The gardens are pleasant, with a small lily pond and lake to the east at the rear of the Hall. Inside, the entrance hall with its Corinthian columns leads into a series of fine, well lit rooms, some of which contain family portraits. The best are those of the family in the 17th century. They give the impression that at that time they were at their most vigorous, which is strengthened by their active role in the Civil War. However, a son of the Civil War Edward Mainwaring, led his tenants against the invading Scots Highlanders in 1745. The last notable owner of the house was Admiral Rowland Mainwaring, who fought under Nelson at the Battle of the Nile and the Battle of Copenhagen.

Perhaps the most interesting feature of the estate is the Tudor stable block which is part of a block of service buildings twenty yards to the north of the house. Stone built with a small cupola, the building clearly contains stalls for horses, but displays no evidence of a door big enough for horses to enter.

Wightwick Manor

WHERE
Map reference SO 865985; on the A454 to Bridgnorth 3 miles west of Wolverhampton. The turn is badly signposted; look for Wightwick Bank.

TRANSPORT
Buses pass; enquiries; 0121 200 2700.

ACCESS & FACILITIES
The Manor is owned by the National Trust; get details of opening and admission prices on 01902 761108. The house is very popular and access is restricted by ticket. There is a cafeteria, the inevitable National Trust shop and WCs, and a small car park.

HISTORY
Victorian houses are rarely of great interest but Wightwick Manor is a triumphant exception. This late Victorian Arts and Crafts house was built by the Wolverhampton paint maker, Theodore Mander. Work began in 1887 at the height of the movement

Wightwick Manor, Wolverhampton

and it is a superb recreation of a mediaeval half timbered manor
house. More, it houses a superb collection of William Morris
fabrics, wallpapers and furnishings, period furniture, tiles,
oriental rugs and porcelain, and pre-Raphaelite pictures. When
the late Lady Mander lived here, Wightwick was very definitely
a home. Now the National Trust has taken full control, I hope
they keep the domestic atmosphere and not turn it into a museum.

The Introduction to the guidebook is a beguiling, idiosyncratic
memoir by Anthea Mander Lahr which recalls life in the house
from 1937, when her parents gave it to the National Trust. She
writes that its remarkable state of preservation is due to the early
deaths of her grandparents in 1900 and 1905, and to the ambivalent
feelings of her father's two wives, who fled to London at the first
opportunity. The house was never modified, never redecorated
and only a few rooms were lived in, making it an exceptional
survival of the Arts and Crafts movement of the 1880s and 90s.

The house was built in 1887 by Theodore Mander and his wife,
Flora St Clair Paint. They bought part of the Wightwick Estate,
renovated the Tudor manor house and buildings and hired Edward
Ould to build a new house. He was an expert in the "Old English"
style of half timbered building in stone and brick. In 1893 he
added an entire half timbered East Wing, a careful re-creation
of a late mediaeval manor house which doubled the size of the
building.

The house has not been altered since it was built, but was much
enhanced by Theodore Mander's son, Sir Geoffrey and his wife,
the Pre-Raphaelite expert Rosalie Glynn Grylls. They compiled an
outstanding collection of Pre-Raphaelite pictures and added a great
deal of work from the Morris firm and other producers of Arts and
Crafts material. In 1937 they presented Wightwick to the National
Trust, its first acquisition under the Country House Scheme. The
Manders continued to live there until Sir Geoffrey died in 1962 and
Lady Mander in 1988. In 1989-91 the domestic wing was restored
and the family retain close links with the house. In recent years a
programme of restoration has added to the areas open to the public
the Kitchen and Servants quarters. The day and night nurseries,
Edwardian and 1930s, have been restored and were opened for
the first time in 1991.

DESCRIPTION
Despite appearances Wightwick is emphatically a late 19th century
house and not a mediaeval one; the genuine mediaeval house, the
old Manor, is today used as a tea room and shop. In the main house,

the central heating and electric light, which was installed from the first, and the bright red, wire cut brick in the early section, show that this is a recreation, not a reconstruction.

Wightwick's original decoration was not directly supervised by William Morris or his firm, but Morris wallpapers, furnishings and fittings are mixed with de Morgan tiles and WAS Benson metalwork. There is also plasterwork by Leonard Shuffrey and stained glass by Charles Kempe. The interior layout and furnishing is far too rich to cover properly in a brief description, but I must mention the Great Parlour. This grand room is modelled on a Tudor Great Hall, complete with Minstrels gallery. While the effect is mediaeval, the date 1893 is carved above the fire place, and a kangaroo appears in the Elizabethan style frieze.

The pictures are a very fine collection which it is difficult to appreciate on the standard tour of the house. Look out for Millais's famous picture of Effie Ruskin - later his wife, which is in the Upper Hall. In the Drawing Room she appears again drawn by G F Watts, and his picture of Jane Hughes hangs the Great Parlour. Burne Jones's painting *Love Among the Ruins* in the Great Parlour is also well thought of, though his androgynous figures are a matter of taste.

The seventeen acre garden was designed by Thomas Mawson in the 1900s as a setting for the Manor. Formal gardens are laid out in a framework of terraces and stone walls with topiary. Beyond are informal areas with two orchards, banks of shrubs and trees, and a stream which fills tranquil fish pools.

Wilderhope Manor

WHERE
Map reference SJ 545929; 7.5 miles south-west of Much Wenlock on the B4371 near Longville in the Dale.

TRANSPORT
Buses may be sighted occasionally; enquiries 01743 253030.

ACCESS & FACILITIES
The Manor is owned by the National Trust but occupied as a Youth Hostel. Access is restricted, but phone 01694 771363 for details of opening hours. There is no NT shop, WCs or refreshments; for those items visit the Longville Arms, Longville in the Dale.

HISTORY

Like Shipton Manor a mile away, Wilderhope Manor is a classic
Elizabethan stone manor house. Both were built when this remote
west Shropshire valley of Corvedale was one of the prosperous
and advanced areas of England. Unlike Shipton, Wilderhope was
never cherished and extended, little was spent on it, and by the
mid 20th century it stood abandoned and derelict. Fortunately it
was rescued and and restored by the Cadbury Trust and National
Trust. You can visit is as a most interesting example of an Elizabethan manor house almost unaffected by changing fashion. It was
the model for Undern Hall in Mary Webb's book, *Gone to Earth.*

The lands at Wilderhope were bought in 1583 by Thomas Smallman and leased to his younger brother, Francis. Francis built the
present house. His initials and those of his wife, Ellen, appear
repeatedly on the ceiling plasterwork. The building remained
in the Smallman family until 1742 when it was sold to Thomas
Lutwyche. He was a descendant of Richard Lutwyche who had
built Shipton Hall in 1587. The similarities between Wilderhope
and Shipton are so pronounced that the same builder must have
been responsible. They share the same broad gables, none of
them precisely the same width or depth, the same asymmetrical
front, and the same odd feature of a totally detached pediment
floating above the archway of the entrance. Like Shipton Hall,
Wilderhope is also built of the local Aymestry limestone, though
the tall chimney stacks are in beautifully executed brickwork.

The building was owned by the Lutwyche family from 1742 until
the 19th century, when it was sold and used as a farmhouse. By
the early 20th century it was on the verge of demolition when the
Cadbury Trust stepped in. The roof was leaking, one of the chimneys had fallen down, windows had been bricked up. Repairs were
started in 1936 and the house was turned into a Youth Hostel,
an ideal use since no major alterations were needed beyond
installing a hot water system.

DESCRIPTION

Wilderhope Manor stands on the flank of Wenlock Edge facing
south-east. The external walls, are of small uncoursed rubble with
dressed quoins and up to four and a half feet thick in some places.
It is hard to see why such a structure was needed in a house which
was not fortified. The interior walls are timber framed with wattle
and daub infill. The roof is supported on oak and chestnut timbers
and clad with stone tiles, the chimneys are brick. Wilderhope
Manor is very strongly built, indicating considerable wealth in
those who built it. A notable feature is the main circular

Wilderhope Manor, Shropshire

staircase leading from the ground floor to the attics and capped with
a conical roof. Each step is made from a solid block of wood.

All the original window frames have survived, but only a few of the
mullions on the north-west side. Both mullions and transoms survive
on the main front looking over the valley. The windows give a sense
of order to the irregular design, laying a coating of Renaissance
symmetry over an essentially mediaeval design. The decoration is
austere with a lack of carved ornament or embellishment, in marked
contrast to the roughly contemporary Moreton Corbet Castle fifteen
miles to the north. Wilderhope was the house of local gentry, not
of a family of national consequence and wealth like the Corbetts.
Nothing remains of the original contents apart from the bow rack
above the chimney piece in the hall. With space for thirteen bows,
it is believed to be the largest in existence.

The main feature of Wilderhope Manor is the plasterwork of the
ceilings. Many of the mouldings feature the portcullis, the Tudor
rose, the fleur-de-lys and the word "Jesu" on a heart, which links
Wilderhope to the legend of Prince Arthur's funeral procession.
These motifs were also used at Upton Cressett and Morville Hall,
indicating that the same plasterers were at work, but they do not
appear at Shipton. There is a puzzling feature in a plain shield
carrying the words *droi due est mal meu,* roughly translated
"lawful right should not be interfered with". This also appears
at Easthope Manor, the Abbots House at Buildwas and Belswar-
dyne. It does not seem to have been the Smallman family motto
and its status in the house is unknown.

Landmark Trust

The Landmark Trust is a charity with two interlocking purposes. The first is to save worthwhile buildings and their surroundings from neglect. The second is to promote enjoyment of such places, mainly by letting them for holidays. Such use has the advantage over mere conservation on the National Trust or English Heritage model of making the buildings lived in, as well as raising income for their upkeep. This special section covers a selection of these unusual buildings with comparatively brief entries. Not all of them were "power houses" as outlined in the *Introduction,* but they are certainly fascinating and worth knowing.

Information about the Trust and its lettings policy can be obtained from its office at Shottesbrooke, Maidenhead, Berkshire SL6 3SW. Phone 01628 825925, Fax 01628 825417. There are five Landmark properties in the area covered by this book. This does not imply that they are open at any particular time. As with most private property, they are not normally open to the public except by prior arrangement, though you can peer at some of them from the road.

Ingestre Pavillion

WHERE
Map reference SJ 981245; like the house whose gardens it occupies, The Pavilion at Ingestre is very hard to find. Ingestre House is a mile north of Tixall and 3.6 miles east of Stafford. There are no signs.

HISTORY
The Pavilion was built at Ingestre Hall by the Chetwynds who were enlightened patrons of architecture. So also were the Talbots who later owned the house, and later still, Alton Towers. The Pavilion was erected in 1752, probably by a local mason/architect named Charles Trubshaw. It has a powerful and distinguished classical facade with four classical columns supporting a wide, low, triangular pediment. The building behind was originally a large and grand place, but though it survived Capability Brown's landscaping of the Park in 1756, the rooms were demolished in 1802. leaving only the facade.

The Talbots sold Ingestre Hall to Sandwell Borough Council for use as an educational centre; they sold the facade to Landmark. The Trust hired the architect Philip Jebb to rebuild the pavilion. He created an octagonal saloon used as a living room, with a bedroom, kitchen and toilets letting off it and two bedrooms and a bathroom above. The Pavilion sleeps up to six people, with two twins and a double bed. It provides an ideal base near to Cannock Chase.

Langley Gatehouse

WHERE
Map reference SJ 537000. The Landmark Trust guide notes that this building is difficult to find. Indeed it is. Find Acton Burnell Castle which is 7.5 miles south-east of Shrewbury between the A49 and A458. Here, look for the English Heritage sign to Langley Chapel, which is 1 mile to the south, and ask for directions from locals. It is worth the trip for this charming, remote, sheep filled Shropshire valley.

HISTORY
The Gatehouse too is worth finding, for it is a splendid example of a half timbered Jacobean gatehouse, much more impressive than the Old Hall Gatehouse at Maevsyn Ridware, and as splendid in its way as the stone one at Tixall near Stafford. It was built as the entrance to Langley Hall (demolished by 1880), and appears to have survived as a farm outbuilding. It has two fronts. The outer one of stone once formed the entrance, but now faces the muck and machinery of a farmyard. The inner front is half timbered with two splendid gables, and provides the main front of the Landmark property. In the next field is the Langley Chapel, a simple one roomed puritan church of the Elizabethan period.

The Gatehouse was built by Sir Humphrey Lee in about 1610, though part of the stone wall is much older. It probably housed the steward or important guests. The parlour over the Gate passage was panelled with a moulded plaster cornice. The roof itself is made from moss covered Harnage stone slates, thick with fossilised shells. It was very near collapse when Landmark and English Heritage began repairs in 1992, work admirably done by Treasures of Ludlow. For escaping from it all, a stay at the Gatehouse with its view of a sheep lined valley facing the far distant Wrekin could hardly be bettered. It accommodates up to six people.

Tixall Gatehouse

WHERE
Map reference SJ 979231; 4 miles east of Stafford on the Stafford to
Great Haywood road.

HISTORY
This magnificent Tudor gatehouse is the more strange and arresting
because it now stands alone in a field. It was built around 1580 by
Sir Walter Austin, but the house which stood behind it has long
gone, and so has a successor built in 1780. In their place stands
an incongruous row of semicircular mews dwellings.

However, there is nothing incongruous about Tixall Gatehouse,
in spite of its odd position and the small size of its gate opening
compared to its bulk. The Gatehouse was meant to express wealth
and power to people on the nearby road, who could not see the
house because it stood behind a wall. It succeeds triumphantly.
Four ogee topped towers proudly guard the corners as the Gatehouse stands tall and stately, commanding a vista of Tixall Wide.
This small scenic lake in the Staffordshire & Worcestershire
Canal is said to have been recommended by Capability Brown;
there are few things like it on any other canal.

The Landmark Trust bought the Gatehouse in 1968 and made five
visitor's rooms on the first floor. Its centre is a gallery, now used
as a drawing room, with oriel windows over the gate archways at
each end. The Trust rightly remarks that "the roof is paved with
stone, and to be high up here among the balustrades and turret tops,
with Arcadian landscape on every hand, is an important Landmark
Trust experience". Typically, while the clock in one of the turrets
chimes the hour and half hour, it has no hands.

Alton Station

WHERE
Map reference SK 072427; by the River Churnet at Alton which is
on the B5032 between Cheadle and Rocester. [see also - Alton
Towers and Alton Castle]

HISTORY

The Landmark Trust does not just care for ancient houses, and Alton railway station is one of its more unusual properties. This is the only Italianate style railway station in Staffordshire and was built in 1849 by the famous North Staffordshire Railway, or (from its Staffordshire knot emblem) the "Knotty". The line carried passengers to Alton Towers and the station was set up in a manner befitting one used by the Earl of Shrewsbury. It stands in marvellous surroundings. Pugin's Alton Castle rises out of the trees across the Churnet Valley, while to the north lies Alton Towers with its famous garden, and even more famous and noisy theme park.

The railway has gone, but in its day it carried twelve carriage excursion trains from Stoke and elsewhere to Alton Towers. The housekeeper, Mrs Bowers, was one of the last people to travel on the line and still has her ticket from Leek to Alton, dated 2nd January 1965. The property sleeps up to six people, with two bedrooms one on top of another in an Italianate tower.

34, High Street, Ironbridge

WHERE

Map reference SJ 673035; on the north bank of the River Severn facing the Iron Bridge.

HISTORY

Number 34 High Street, Ironbridge is a complete and unique house built by a wealthy grocer. Mr Smith specially placed his home and business on the crowded, precipitous east flank of the Ironbridge Gorge. It is a large house over a double fronted shop with offices and stores behind. From the cellars a tunnel runs to the banks of the River Severn so that stock could be carried from barges. The river was navigable until the late 19th century. A special feature of the house is that it overlooks Abraham Darby's famous Iron Bridge, the first in the world and a harbinger of the Industrial Revolution.

The shop is let to the Ironbridge Gorge Museum Trust. Mr Smith's quarters upstairs are divided in two, one part is let to a long term tenant, the other to the Trust. The living room has an iron freplace which was cast at Coalbrookdale in the Gorge, as were the bathroom basin and lavatory cistern. Every room faces the Gorge, the Iron Bridge and the steep wooded bank beyond.

Further Reading

Life in the English Country House by Mark Girouard, Penguin 1980

The Decline of the Castle by M W Thompson, Magna Books 1987

A Guide to the English Country House by Garry Hayes, Country Life 1966

Historic Gardens by Jane Fearnley Whittington, Grange Books 1993

The Glory of the English Country House by Lionel Esher, Barrie & Jackson 1991

Shire County Guide 11 - Staffordshire by Peter Heaton, Shire Books 1986

A Love Affair with Nature by Edwin Mullins, Phaidon 1985

The Buildings of England - Shropshire by Nicklaus Pevsner, Penguin 1958

... ditto ... - Staffordshire, 1974

Architecture in Britain 1530 - 1830 by John Summerson, Penguin 1991

Polite Landscapes by Tom Williamson, Alan Sutton Publishing 1995

The Story of Architecture by Patrick Nuttgens, Phaidon 1983